Editorial Project Manager
Jodi L. McClay, M.A.

Editorial Manager
Karen J. Goldfluss, M.S. Ed.

Editor in Chief
Sharon Coan, M.S. Ed.

Illustrator
Wendy Chang

Cover Artist
Denise Bauer

Art Coordinator
Cheri Macoubrie Wilson

Creative Director
Elayne Roberts

Imaging
Ralph Olmedo, Jr.
James Edward Grace

Product Manager
Phil Garcia

Publishers
Rachelle Cracchiolo, M.S. Ed.
Mary Dupuy Smith, M.S. Ed.

Teaching Reading Across the Curriculum

Author

Mary Riordan-Karlsson, Ed. D.

Teacher Created Materials, Inc.
6421 Industry Way
Westminster, CA 92683
www.teachercreated.com
ISBN-1-57690-466-0
©*1999 Teacher Created Materials, Inc.*
Made in U.S.A.

Table of Contents

Introduction

Teaching Reading Across the Curriculum is designed to assist teachers in addressing reading skills and strategies in all content areas. The focus of this book is on content area reading and writing strategies, which appear to be strongly needed by teachers. Specific reading, writing, and study strategies will be discussed using examples of lessons and activities within units from across the curriculum. Each unit integrates reading and writing activities in the content areas. This resource book will remind teachers how important it is to integrate reading, writing, and learning in the middle grades in all content areas.

Teaching Reading Across the Curriculum describes the importance of reading and writing in the content areas; however, it exceeds the use of reading and writing skills or tools in other content areas, such as social science, mathematics, science, and the fine arts. We now know that reading and writing are essential elements in the learning process. Current theories of the reading and learning process reveal that learning in the content areas involves more than utilizing tools and skills with content area texts (Ruddell and Ruddell, 1995). More accurately, learners negotiate and construct meaning in the very act of reading and writing, building on their prior knowledge, negotiating ideas, integrating new information, and constructing new content area knowledge. The constructions of meanings and negotiations occur before, during, and after reading and writing events. As students interact and transact with texts (Rosenblatt, 1978), comprehension levels improve, and it is these constructions of knowledge that form the basis for content area learning.

 **Reading and writing are essential elements in the learning process.**

In the past, content area writing focused on informational reports, lab reports, essays, or research papers. Students used writing skills to accomplish their goals but were not integrating writing and learning. Today we know that writing is also an essential element in the learning process and writing serves as a way of learning. It is through the act of writing that students' ideas evolve and change. Writer's workshop, made famous by Donald Graves (1983), Nancie Atwell (1990), and Lucie Calkins (1994), has taught us that when children are engaged in the process of writing, a higher level of learning occurs. As children become authors and live the "writerly life" as Calkins (1994) describes, new ideas emerge and new meanings are constructed. In this book you will find many opportunities to engage students in the act of writing and learning.

We want our students to become active learners, therefore, we must offer effective strategies that will engage students and encourage them to become active participants in the learning process, which means more than just using study skills. The instructional strategies discussed in this book have the study skills, such as understanding parts of a book, notetaking, outlining, and summarizing, embedded in them, so these skills play a natural role in the learning process. Study skills should not be taught in isolation; they should be embedded in instructional strategies and planning.

Introduction *(cont.)*

Teaching Reading Across the Curriculum offers a variety of effective strategies that will motivate your students to become actively engaged in learning. The lessons and activities in each unit illustrate how these strategies fit into your curriculum. Content area learning through the promotion of rich reading and writing experiences is the ultimate goal.

In order for content area learning to occur, we are asking a great deal of our students. Ruddell and Ruddell (1995) state that we are asking them to engage in the entire learning process. Before engaging in a learning event, students need to recall prior knowledge and previous experience, identify what they know, raise questions about what they do not know, and predict what the test or evaluation will be about.

Students also need to organize information while reading, predict what information will be found, revise predictions, and relate new information to prior knowledge. We also want our students to learn vocabulary that labels important concepts, elements, and relationships, identify new words and terms, identify known words and terms in new contexts, use new words and terms in meaningful ways, and relate new vocabulary to a prior knowledge base.

After the learning event, we expect our students to respond to text in some important way, identify major concepts and ideas, perceive relationships among concepts and ideas, perceive relationships with prior knowledge, and understand the relative importance of ideas. In groups or individually, we expect our students to synthesize and articulate new learning, arrive at new understandings and insights, integrate new understandings into a prior knowledge base, find out how much was learned, and establish a base for further learning. Finally, we require our students to produce or create something new, apply new information, and work through new ideas in writing. They should also build, make, create something new, or perform.

Since we expect so much of our students it is only fair that we should expect a great deal from ourselves. As we plan to implement a variety of content area learning strategies into our instructional plan, we need to determine students' prior knowledge and previous experiences concerning the specific topic, provide means for students to articulate their prior knowledge bases, find out what students already know, and determine the magnitude of difference between what students know and what is to be learned (Ruddell and Ruddell, 1995). We can assist our students in the quest for knowledge and information by providing a means for students to organize information while reading, focussing students' attention, engaging students in the cycle of predicting, reading, adjusting predictions, reading some more, and developing linkages between prior knowledge and new information.

The activities and lessons presented in this book are just suggested guides and can be adapted to any level from third grade through eighth grade. Use your judgment and your own curriculum to guide your planning and instruction. Many of the lessons and activities can be done in an electronic form on the computer as a way to integrate technology into your curriculum. It is hoped that *Teaching Reading Across the Curriculum* will be a resource for you to create an exciting and motivating classroom learning environment. Your students will be actively engaged in literacy events that encourage negotiation of meaning and the construction of new ideas.

Introduction *(cont.)*

The book is divided into three sections. In the first section, step-by-step explanations of content reading strategies are offered, and in the second section, these strategies are integrated into content area units and lessons. Generic forms that can be used with any content area unit and a bibliography are provided in the third section.

══════════════════ **Section I** ══════════════════

❏ Content Reading Strategies

Content Directed Reading-Thinking Activity (Content DR-TA)—This activity gives students the opportunity to begin to organize prior knowledge and new knowledge learned during the literacy event (Stauffer, 1969, 1976).

Group Mapping Activity (GMA)—In this activity students analyze and synthesize information from text, using study maps, story clusters, or webs (Davidson, 1982).

Teaching Vocabulary in Context (TVC)—This strategy is used to introduce vocabulary before reading a text as well as a follow-up activity for reinforcement (Ruddell and Ruddell, 1995).

Vocabulary Self-Collection Strategy (VSS)—Students nominate one or two topic-specific words or terms the class should learn or know more about; the teacher also nominates two to three words. The words are contextually situated (Haggard, 1985, 1989; Ruddell, 1993).

Vocabulary Log or Journal—Students keep a log of vocabulary words learned throughout the different lessons and units.

Word Sleuthing—For this activity students become word sleuths and investigate words in their vocabulary logs.

K-W-L Plus Worksheet—This is a worksheet students fill out before, during, and after a unit of study. The letter K stands for what the student already knows, the W represents what the student wants to know, and the L indictates what the students learned. The "Plus" refers to the mapping activity (Carr & Ogle, 1987).

Directed Inquiry Activity (DIA)—The teacher develops a list of inquiry questions about the text to be read and the students preview the text to make predictions. After reading the text, students reexamine inquiry questions and refine responses (Thomas, 1986).

Concept Webs—This strategy involves the use of a simple map used to develop and connect key concepts with a student's prior knowledge and information in the text.

Semantic Maps—These are graphic representations of information which can include general or specific terms used before reading to activate the student's background knowledge or after reading to help the student summarize and integrate ideas.

Semantic Feature Analysis (SFA)—A grid is constructed for a concept (elements or exemplars are listed vertically, and features of one or more exemplars are listed horizontally) and can be filled in as a story is read or a unit is developed.

Introduction (cont.)

Question-Answer Relationship (QAR)—This is a strategy in which students are encouraged to understand the thinking processes involved in developing answers to different types of questions (Raphael, 1982). The four types of questions include: right there, think and search, author and you, and on my own.

Reading Response Groups—Students work in small groups and the teacher provides prompts to guide response group discussions on content-specific texts. Students share group responses in whole-class discussion (O'Flahavan, 1989; Farnan, 1992).

❑ Content Writing Strategies

Journal Writing—This strategy involves free-form or structured writing using content specific prompts in a personal and confidential journal. Journals allow children to record their thoughts and opinions and work out confusions about topics in a conversational manner.

Learning Logs—Learning logs are a special kind of journal for students to record brainstorming ideas from DR-TAs or K-W-L Plus, or to create concept maps (Blake, 1990; Chard, 1990).

Double-Entry Journals (DEJs)—This is another special kind of journal where the student uses the left page for initial responses to prompts or drawings and the right page for revised ideas or new insights (Vaughn, 1990).

Beginning Researchers—This writing strategy encourages students to become researchers and to move away from the informational report writing mode. There are three phases to the program: phase one is taking notes and developing research ideas from listening, phase two is reading and taking notes, and phase three is initiating and carrying out research (Maxim, 1990).

Guided Writing (Expressive Writing)—This type of writing encourages students to think about content area topics through expressive writing (Prenn & Honeychurch, 1990).

Section II

The second section provides the teacher with the following content area units:

- **Ancient Egypt**
- **Ancient Greece**
- **The Olympic Games**
- **Westward Expansion**
- **World War II**
- **The Rain Forest**

Each unit integrates a number of reading and writing strategies into the lessons and activites.

Section I
Step-by-Step
Strategies

Content Directed Reading-Thinking Activity (DR-TA)

The content directed reading-thinking activity (Stauffer, 1976) encourages students to make predictions based on background knowledge and experiences and then evaluate the predictions after reading the text selection. The teacher directs the students to first think about the topic and then read the text. The approach involves active comprehension and exchange of students' ideas which are the result of higher-level thinking types of questions. Students are asked to predict, analyze, and evaluate information which are all higher-level thinking skills. The content directed reading-thinking activity is most effective when students work with partners or in small groups with a designated recorder, so they can discuss and negotiate ideas and meanings.

Strategy for Partner or Group Work

1. Ask students/teams to brainstorm for ten minutes and list everything they know about a general topic, such as World War II or the rain forest.

2. Announce the specific topic of the lesson and direct the students' attention to that topic, such as animals that live in the rain forest.

3. Ask students to review their lists and predict what information will appear in the text by checking off the items (✓).

4. Have students add new ideas to their lists now that they know the specific topic.

5. Have students read the assigned text individually and evaluate their predictions by circling the correct items they have on their lists.

6. Lead a short class discussion about what the students knew before they read the text and what new information they learned. Ask such questions as "How well did you predict? What was something you knew before we read this selection? What new information did you learn after you read this selection?"

Group Mapping Activity (GMA)

The group mapping activity builds comprehension as students integrate and synthesize information, ideas, and concepts (Davidson, 1982). This activity is most effective after students have read a text selection and can use what they learned to create study maps. The GMA strategy invites students to create graphic representations of their personal interpretations of the relationships among ideas and concepts from the text. This representation can take the form of a map or diagram using circles, squares, other shapes, lines, or words depicting their own understanding of the text. Emphasize that there is no right or wrong way to create this map. Once students have completed their maps, they can share them in small groups or with the whole class. It is during this sharing time that students' ideas and understandings are elaborated on or extended.

Strategy for Group Mapping

1. Prepare a sample map to show students.

2. After reading the text and before talking with a classmate or looking back at the text selection, the students should individually map what they believe to be the important concepts and ideas from the text selection.

3. Remind students that their maps will be used throughout the unit of study and should include all information they feel is significant.

4. Have children share their maps with partners or in small groups.

5. Remind students to explain what they chose to include, how they chose to design their maps, and why they made their specific choices.

6. Have students work collaboratively with partners or in small groups to finish their maps.

7. Encourage students to review the text to clarify questions or information.

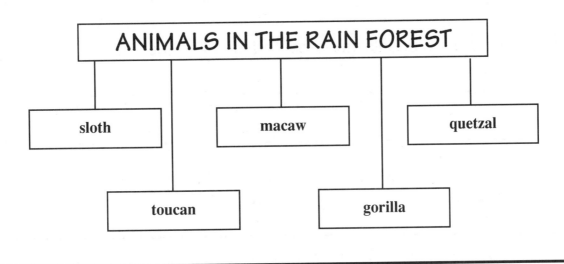

Teaching Vocabulary in Context (TVC)

Teaching vocabulary in context before reading the text selection is an effective strategy to introduce vocabulary because it accesses prior knowledge and experiences. When identifying the new vocabulary to teach, take into consideration the background knowledge bases of your students, concepts and ideas central to the text selection, and the readability of the text. Introduce the vocabulary terms during the introduction to the story and discuss those words that are central to fully understanding the text selection. This strategy may also be used to assess your students' vocabulary knowledge and determine the need for follow-up activities.

1. Preview the text selection to select four or five content-specific vocabulary words to be taught during the lesson.

2. Display the words in sentences on a chart so students can refer to them and recognize context clues as they read the text selection.

3. Read the sentence aloud and have students guess what they think the word means.

4. Record the students' guesses and ideas on the chart.

5. Agree on a definition by checking a dictionary or glossary, if necessary.

Vocabulary Self-Collection Strategy (VSS)

The purpose of the vocabulary self-collection strategy is to encourage long-term acquisition and development of vocabulary (Haggard, 1982; 1986; Ruddell, 1993). The two major characteristics of the VSS strategy are as follows: (1) the strategy focuses on words or terms that are important to students, words they want and need to know, and (2) it encourages students to become independent word learners during their own life experiences. Students have the opportunity to nominate words relevant to the text they feel are important to add to the class vocabulary list. This strategy also includes follow-up activities to reinforce the definitions of words and terms.

Follow-Up Activities

1. After reading or writing a text selection, ask students to work in pairs or small groups to identify a word or term they would like to learn more about.

2. Prepare students to explain where they found the word in the text and read the sentence aloud, guess what the word means, and explain why they think it is important to learn and why it should be on the class vocabulary list.

3. Accept word nominations and lead a discussion of possible meanings and reasons for adding it to the class vocabulary list. Encourage students to negotiate meanings and collaborate to refine the meaning of the word or term.

4. Nominate words or terms you want to add to the list and offer explanations (step #2 above).

5. If there are too many words, narrow the list down by taking a class vote.

6. Refine definitions of words and terms, if needed.

7. Have students write the final list of words and definitions in their vocabulary journals or study maps. The words that were not chosen to be on the final list may still be recorded in each student's personal vocabulary journal.

8. Plan and develop extension activities to reinforce words or terms.

9. Provide time for students to complete the extension activities or projects.

10. Integrate vocabulary words into appropriate assessment activites for the unit of study.

The VSS strategy focuses on important words and terms.

The VSS strategy encourages students to become independent word learners.

Vocabulary Log or Journal

Vocabulary logs or journals provide an efficient method for students to record and learn new words, terms, and concepts. Entries may come from the vocabulary self-collection strategy, class discussions, free-reading materials, or personal conversations. The log or journal may include photographs or illustrations of words and concepts, sentences containing the words, and other pertinent notes. Students can also record word connections and relationships through graphic representations, concept webs, semantic maps, or semantic feature analyses. The journal can be organized according to alphabetical order, chronological order or subject matter, or even a combination of approaches. Student-created journal folders or three-ring binders can be used to collect many of the writing and vocabulary activities in this book. An electronic document file (on the computer) may also be used as an efficient method of recording vocabulary.

Log or Journal Strategy

1. Explain that throughout the year students will be responsible for efficiently recording new words, terms, and concepts related to content area text selections. This collection of words, terms, or concepts will be an individual task as well as a class activity.

2. Encourage students to create graphic representations of connections and relationships among words, terms, and concepts in the units of study.

3. Respond (optional) to journal entries by writing comments and suggestions in the margin to provide feedback to students as their vocabularies develop.

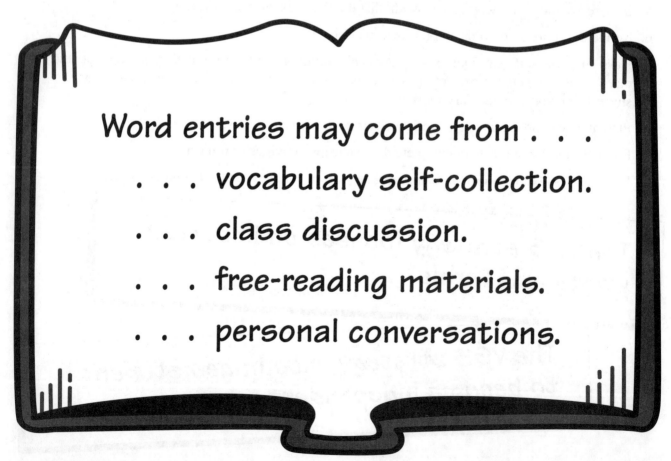

Word entries may come from . . .

. . . vocabulary self-collection.

. . . class discussion.

. . . free-reading materials.

. . . personal conversations.

Word Sleuthing

This activity encourages students to become word sleuths and investigate the origins and meanings of words, terms, phrases, word families, and concepts. Students are invited to also collect words from their home environment and they identify words found in newspaper articles, television or radio shows, advertisements, or on the Internet. Through this activity, students are motivated to investigate vocabulary words and concepts, and the vocabulary logs or journals provide a method of collection and recording.

Word-Sleuthing Strategy

1. Explain that students will be "word sleuths." The student's job is to investigate the origins and meanings of words, terms, phrases, word families, and concepts related to units of study in your class.

2. Ask students to conduct investigations into words borrowed from other languages and cultures. This will build vocabulary interest.

3. Have students investigate new words, such as *online* or *floppy,* and new meanings related to technology. They can collect and examine these new terms.

K-W-L Plus Worksheet

The K-W-L Plus worksheet is very similar to a combination of the content DR-TA and the group mapping activity. There are two parts to this strategy: (1) the K-W-L worksheet and (2) a map generated from the K-W-L worksheet (Carr and Ogle, 1987). In this strategy, the K stands for what students already know, the W represents what students want to know, and the L reflects information that students have learned. The term "Plus" refers to the mapping activity that is part of this strategy. Students can design their own K-W-L worksheets and maps and use them in their portfolios.

The K-W-L Strategy

1. Ask students to work individually, in partners, or in small groups to brainstorm and list everything they know about a specific topic in the first column, the "K" column.

2. Have students fill out the "W" column and list what they want to know about the specific topic.

3. Have students individually read the text selection and complete the last column on the worksheet, the "L" column, and summarize what they have learned.

4. Have students use the information from their K-W-L worksheets to create maps to display the new knowledge they have learned from the text selection.

K	W	L
What I Know	**What I Want to Know**	**What I Learned**
• fly • have wings and feathers • different colors and sizes	• What do they eat? • Do they sleep? • How do they live out in the cold?	• Some birds migrate when seasons change.

Directed Inquiry Activity (DIA)

The directed inquiry activity (Thomas, 1986) is similar to the content DR-TA and the K-W-L Plus strategy as it encourages students to connect prior knowledge with new knowledge through predictions and follow-up responses. Before students read the text selection, the teacher previews it and selects four or five inquiry questions to ask students. These questions help students make predictions. After students read the selection, they can revise their responses and decide on answers that require further inquiry.

Strategy for Directed Inquiry

1. Decide on lesson objectives and then write four or five inquiry questions that relate to those objectives.

2. Choose which sections of the text the students should preview and identify specific text features they should pay attention to, such as chapter headings, marginal notes, charts, and graphs.

3. Record the inquiry questions on a chart, white/black board, or on a student worksheet. Make sure you leave enough room for students to record their predictions and other responses.

4. Have students preview the reading assignment and make predictions based on their responses to the inquiry questions.

5. Lead a class discussion to provide the opportunity for students to share their predictions. Make sure students discuss their reasoning and logic for their responses.

6. Have students read the assigned text selection.

7. Lead a student discussion to reexamine the responses to the inquiry questions and add new knowledge and information. In small or large groups, students develop additional inquiry questions.

8. Assign follow-up activities such as the group mapping activity or the vocabulary self-collection strategy.

Concept Webs

The concept web strategy encourages students to create a diagram or map used to develop and connect students' prior knowledge, understandings, and experiences with information found in the text selection. Concept webs are an important strategy for students to use to integrate knowledge and new information. This strategy can be used as an introductory activity to a unit of study or as a summarization activity.

Concept Web Strategy

1. Write the main concept on a chart, board, or piece of paper.

2. Identify and list ideas and concepts related to the main concept. Draw connecting lines from the main concept to the related concepts and ideas.

3. Have students explain the relationships among the main concept and the other ideas and concepts.

4. Continue to add to the concept web throughout the unit of study.

Sample Survival Web

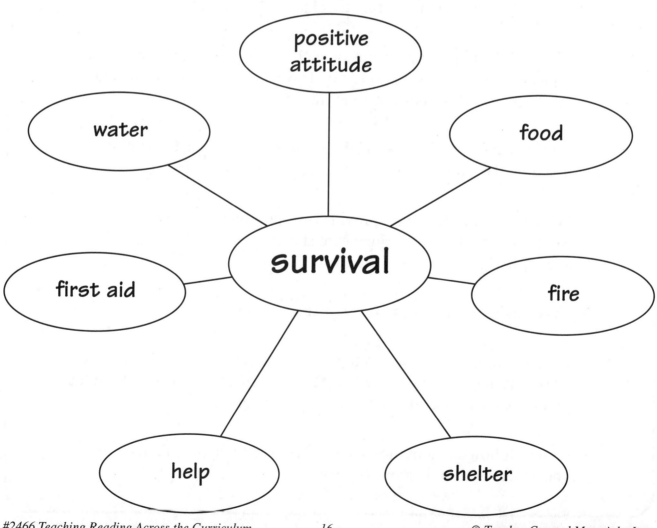

Semantic Maps

Semantic maps are similar to concept webs but require students to discover and identify more complex relationships. Semantic maps are graphic representations that encourage students to make connections among concepts, story ideas, characters, and other information from the text selection. The map will enable students to understand relationships and connections among topics and details as they read new text selections and retrieve new information. This strategy can be used as a brainstorming activity in the beginning of a unit of study to activate students' prior knowledge and/or as a summarization activity to integrate prior knowledge and new information.

Semantic Map Strategy

1. Introduce the main topic and have students brainstorm ideas and information related to the main topic.

2. Draw a circle around the main topic and draw lines connecting the main topic with secondary information or supporting details.

3. Have students develop categories or classifications for the ideas and concepts for writing reports, essays, or the summarization of a text selection.

4. Have students continue to expand the map as they gain new information and make associations with prior knowledge while they read, research, or discuss various related issues and topics.

5. Encourage students to use different colored pencils or markers to identify prior knowledge and new knowledge as they expand their maps.

6. Remind students to include new vocabulary and concepts from the text selections and research information.

7. Have students use their maps to write reports essays or prepare for oral presentations.

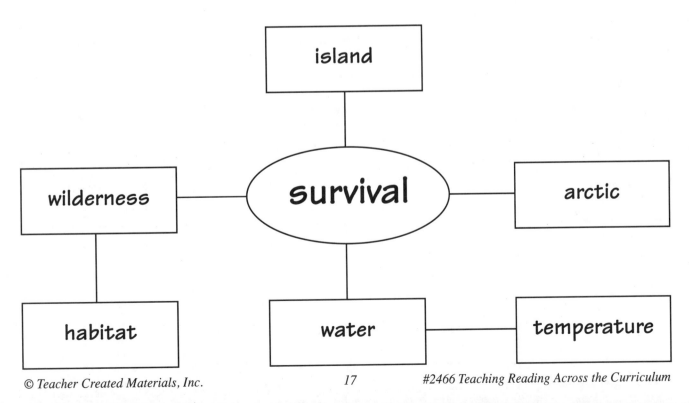

Semantic Feature Analysis (SFA)

A semantic feature analysis is an instructional strategy that helps students develop vocabulary and recognize relationships among words and concepts. The SFA requires students to construct a grid that lists the elements (or vocabulary words) of the concept vertically on the left side with one or more exemplars listed horizontally on the top. Students compare their responses and discuss the similarities and differences found in the grids. This strategy is helpful in teaching students to compare and contrast characters, locations, or settings in stories or text selections. The SFA can be used in all content areas for comparison of various elements.

Semantic Feature Analysis Strategy

1. Decide on elements to be compared and contrasted in the semantic feature analysis.

2. Create a grid that is sized appropriately for the information needed.

3. List the elements of the concept or the vocabulary words vertically on the left side of the grid. The features of one or more of the exemplars are listed horizontally on the top row of the grid.

4. Have students fill in the grid matching the word with the features, marking a positive (+) sign for those features that match and a negative sign (–) for those features that do not match.

5. Have students compare their responses with partners or in small groups and then share them with the whole class.

survival	Dangers			
	animals	weather	weapons	people
wilderness	+	+	–	–
island	–	+	–	+
arctic	+	+	–	+
war	–	–	+	+

Question-Answer Relationship (QAR)

The Question-Answer Relationship strategy (Raphael, 1982) is designed to encourage students to understand the thinking processes and demands of questions and learn how to access information sources in responding to different types of questions. The QAR strategy classifies different types of questions into four categories of information sources: factual, interpretive, applicative, and transactive. This strategy helps students analyze the thinking demands of questions and the processes of developing answers.

In the following categories of question-answer relationships, the first two are "In the Book QARs" and the last two are "In My Head QARs."

- *Right There*—The answer is stated directly in the text and requires simple factual recall.

- *Think and Search*—The answer is in the text but not stated directly. The reader must interpret the meaning and formulate the answer after reading different parts of the text.

- *Author and You*—The answer is not in the text. The reader needs to integrate background knowledge and experiences with information the author provides.

- *On My Own*—The answer is not in the text. The reader must develop the answer based on background knowledge and experiences only.

Implementing the QAR Instructional Strategy

1. Prepare a chart identifying the "In the Book QARs" and "In My head QARs" for students to view.

2. Prepare two short text selections with questions from all four categories.

3. Introduce the QAR chart, explain the illustrations, and give many examples of each category of QAR.

4. Review and practice identifying QARs using the prepared text selections. Have students work with partners or in small groups to read, answer questions, and categorize the questions from the first passage. In whole-class discussion, share group decisions and responses.

5. Have students independently read the second prepared text selection and identify the QARs. Share answers and decisions in a whole-class discussion.

6. Have students select longer text passages, locate QARs in a variety of reading materials, and share them with partners or in small groups.

Reading Response Groups

Similar to literature response groups, reading response groups provide a forum for students to voice their opinions and interpretations of texts, negotiate meanings, and construct new understandings of content. The teacher prepares prompts to guide the response group discussion to focus on specific content in the text selection.

It is recommended that teachers focus on these three areas: (1) background knowledge, (2) ideas derived from the text, (3) ideas that go beyond the text (O'Flahavan, 1989). After students discuss responses to the prompts in small groups, the discussion expands to include the whole class.

Reading Response Group Strategy

1. Decide on the lesson or unit objective.

2. Form reading response groups (either student-selected or teacher-assigned) with four or five students in each group.

3. Review procedures and roles of each participant in a reading response group (recorder, facilitator, or participant).

4. Review the goal of the group and specify the amount of time allotted to answer the prompts.

5. Prepare the reading response group prompts and write them on a chart, board, or on a worksheet.

6. Monitor groups and observe how students are participating and working together. Troubleshoot or clarify prompts, if necessary.

7. Return to large group (or whole-class) discussion and have students share their groups' responses to the prompts. Allow time for students to reflect on and evaluate their responses and the reading response group process.

Areas of Focus

 background knowledge

 ideas derived from the text

 ideas that go beyond the text

Journal Writing

Journal writing provides an opportunity for students to freely write about topics of their choice or units of study in the content areas. Journal writing is a more personalized form of writing, usually involving only the student and the teacher. There are other forms of journal writing, such as learning logs or double-entry journals, that are intended for a public audience. Often, teachers provide prompts for students to brainstorm and free write a response or reaction. Quick Write is a format that encourages students to respond quickly (within three or four minutes) to a question, statement, dialogue, class discussion, or reading passage. Journals allow students to record their thoughts and opinions and work out confusions about various topics, controversial issues, and units of study in a conversational manner.

Journal Writing Strategy

1. Explain the guidelines and the purpose of the journal. For different content areas, the purpose may vary.

2. Remind students that each journal entry should be dated and given a title for easy reference.

3. Provide content-specific prompts for students. Students may react, elaborate, or disagree in their responses.

4. Have students write their responses in their journals with the intent that their teacher will read and respond.

5. Respond to an aspect of a student's entry, not the entire entry. Respond with a question for further student inquiry.

6. Have students use content-specific journals as a study guide for tests and projects.

Learning Logs

The learning log is a specialized form of journals that specifically focuses on content area learning (Blake, 1990; Chard, 1990). Unlike journals, learning logs are not written in a conversational manner. The purpose is for students to record brainstorming ideas from content-directed reading-thinking activities (DR-TAs) or K-W-L Plus worksheets. The learning log is also a great place for students to create concept webs or semantic maps. Most of the writing prompts for students are initiated by the teacher before, during, and after a lesson or unit of study. For easy referance each learning log entry should be dated and given a title.

Learning Logs Strategies

1. Explain the guidelines and the purpose of the learning log. For different content areas, the purpose may vary.

2. Remind students to date and title each entry for easy reference.

3. Provide content-specific prompts or provide procedural prompts for students to respond to, such as "How did your group decide on responses to the questions for the text selection?"

4. Have students write their responses in their learning logs with the intent of using this information to create a concept web, semantic map, or semantic feature analysis. Students can also use their learning logs to brainstorm and make predictions during content directed reading-thinking activities or the K-W-L Plus worksheet strategy.

5. Have students use learning logs as study guides for exams, research projects, or writing assignments.

6. Have students share their learning logs with partners or group members.

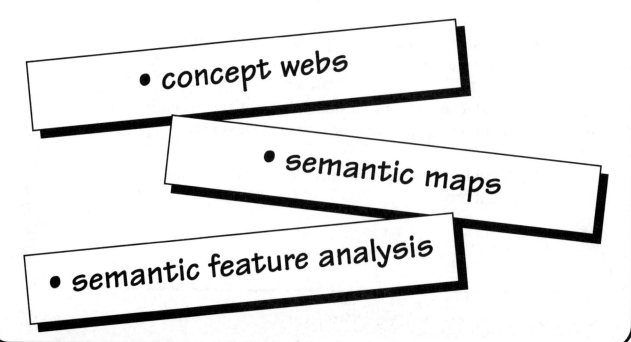

- concept webs
- semantic maps
- semantic feature analysis

Double-Entry Journals (DEJs)

The double-entry journal (Vaughn, 1990) is another form of journal writing that requires students to initially respond to a question, a controversial issue, or a text selection and revise or add onto their ideas after further research. The double-entry journal requires a notebook that allows students to begin with two facing pages. Students can use the left page for initial brainstorming ideas, understandings, interpretations, drawings, maps, or notes. The right page is reserved for refined understandings and interpretations of the information recorded on the left page. Before the literacy activity the students use the left page, and after the activity the students use the right page. Therefore, the student can see how their ideas and understandings evolved. Teachers may provide content-specific prompts for both the left-page and right-page assignments. Double entry journals (DEJs) can be useful guides for content area reading and writing lessons or units and can help students develop and organize their thoughts and ideas.

Double Entry Journals Strategies

1. Have students open their double-entry journals (DEJs) to a new double page (both the left page and right page are blank.)

2. Before a lesson or unit, provide a prompt for a DEJ left-page entry. Students write their reactions, ideas, or interpretations from brainstorming or class discussions on the left page.

3. Encourage students to write everything they know about a specific subject or draw maps or webs.

4. Have students add ideas to the left page throughout the lesson or activity.

5. In the right-page entry, provide a prompt that will encourage students to organize their information into an analysis or summary.

6. Have students share their entries with partners or with the whole class. Students may add information to the right-page entry after discussions.

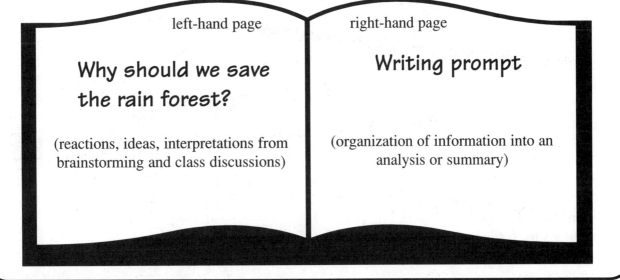

left-hand page

right-hand page

Why should we save the rain forest?

(reactions, ideas, interpretations from brainstorming and class discussions)

Writing prompt

(organization of information into an analysis or summary)

Beginning Researchers

This strategy encourages students to become researchers and to move away from the informational report writing modes (Maxim, 1990). Becoming a beginning researcher helps students access and retrieve information and organize it into an interesting format to present the information to others. There are three phases to the program: *phase one* is taking notes and developing research ideas from listening; *phase two* is reading and taking notes; *phase three* is initiating and carrying out research (Maxim, 1990). This approach to research invites students to focus on a specific unit of study that is concurrently taught in one of their content area classes. Although this strategy requires a good deal of planning by the teacher, it is beneficial to the students to learn how to properly gather and present information in a format other than the traditional informational report.

Research Strategies

1. Decide on a unit of study and specific learning objectives.

2. Gather a variety of resources for students to use to research topics. Plan field trips, schedule guest speakers, and arrange other ways for students to access and retrieve information.

3. Compile a list of text selections related to the unit of study for students to read and use as resources.

4. If necessary, mark the reading passages in the order they should be read.

5. Make sure students have learning logs.

Phase I: Listening and Notetaking

1. To begin the listening and notetaking phase, demonstrate the process by asking students to share their notes and record them on a chart or board. Questions are then generated by the group.

   Do not forget the following procedures:

   - Date and title all learning log entries.

   - Have students record all notes in learning logs after the reading is completed. The notes should consist of facts and details.

   - After their notes, have students write questions and ideas for further research.

2. Continue to read each day different text selections from books related to the unit of study. Each day students should practice listening, taking notes, and generating questions for further research.

Beginning Researchers *(cont.)*

Phase II: Reading and Notetaking

1. Choose a text selection from an informational magazine and makes copies for each student.

2. Distribute the magazine or the copy of the text selection but do not let students read it.

3. Have students predict what the article is about based on the front page. Remind students to record questions in their learning logs.

4. Have students read for ten minutes away from their desks (in the library area, on the rug, at a table or a classmate's desk).

5. After ten minutes, have students stop reading, leave their copies where they are, return to their desks, and take notes from memory. Students write the answers to their questions in their learning logs.

6. In a whole-class discussion ask students to share their notes.

7. Repeat the exercise using a variety of magazines and articles and move to textbook selections when students demonstrate they are ready.

Phase III: Initiating and Carrying Out Research

1. To prepare students for later research in the unit, during Phases I and II provide many opportunities for students to engage in related literacy activities.

2. Encourage students to use other resources within the school and community library, including the reference sections and the Internet.

3. As students progress through the phases and become confident in their notetaking abilities without copying information, encourage students to develop their own research projects related to the unit of study.

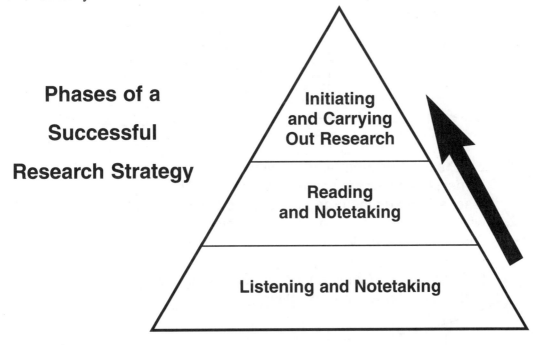

Phases of a Successful Research Strategy

Initiating and Carrying Out Research

Reading and Notetaking

Listening and Notetaking

Guided Writing (Expressive Writing)

The guided writing strategy (Prenn and Honeychurch, 1990) helps students think about content area topics through expressive writing, which is "thinking aloud on paper."

Guided writing provides opportunities for students to connect their prior knowledge, experiences, understandings, and interpretations with content area information. The teacher reads a variety of writing prompts that encourage students to assume roles and imagine scenes in a topic-related mini-drama. The questions within the prompts guide students in the discovery and exploration of the connections between their background knowledge and experiences with feelings and beliefs in relation to the topic.

Guided Writing Strategy

1. Prepare a variety of writing prompts (hypothetical situations) related to the unit of study.

2. Read the series of related writing prompts to students while students assume various roles and imagine the scene.

3. Have students record their answers to the questions within the prompts in their learning logs or journals.

4. After all prompts are read, have students share their answers and ideas with partners in small groups or in a whole-class discussion.

Prenn and Honeychurch (1990) recommend three guidelines for teachers when implementing the guided writing strategy in lessons and units.

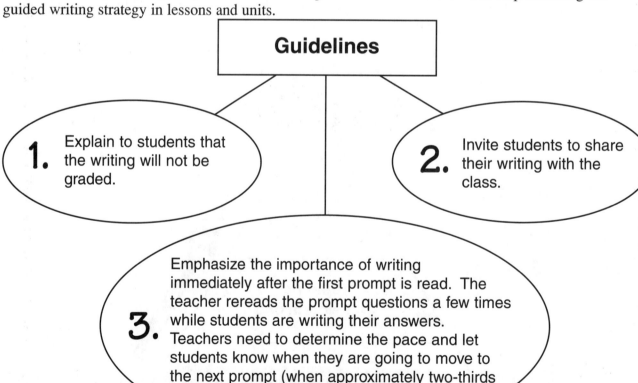

Guidelines

1. Explain to students that the writing will not be graded.

2. Invite students to share their writing with the class.

3. Emphasize the importance of writing immediately after the first prompt is read. The teacher rereads the prompt questions a few times while students are writing their answers. Teachers need to determine the pace and let students know when they are going to move to the next prompt (when approximately two-thirds of the class have finished writing).

Section II

Content Area

Units

Ancient Civilizations

This unit of study on Ancient Civilizations will include activities and lessons on Ancient Egypt, Ancient Greece, and The Olympic Games. Geography, religion, and sports will be the main topics in this unit which will help students to understand and appreciate the way of life many thousands of years ago. Included in this unit of study are individual activities as well as small-group and whole-class activities. Other activities integrate the curriculum areas of social science, mathematics, art, music, reading, writing, and research skills.

A variety of reading and writing strategies can be used within this unit to help students access, retrieve, and organize information. Students will be encouraged to collect information as well as assume the roles of an athlete preparing for the first Olympic Games, an architect for the pyramids, and a famous leader. As students study the history of ancient civilizations they will become actively involved in their learning and "live" the experience through a variety of strategies and lessons. These lessons should be adapted to meet the curriculum and individual needs of your class.

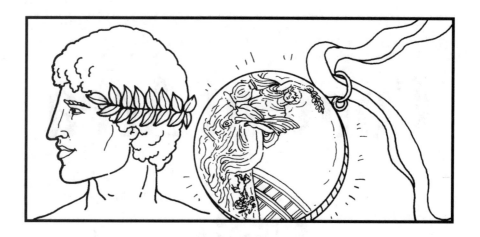

K-W-L Plus Worksheet

Name _____ Date_____

Use this K-W-L Plus worksheet during a class discussion to brainstorm what you know and what you want to know about Ancient Egypt. The third column will be completed at the end of the unit as part of a culminating activity. Here are some topics to consider as you begin your worksheet.

- Cleopatra
- Egyptian pyramids
- King Tut
- Julius Caesar of Rome
- Mark Antony
- Greco-Roman Period

For this activity you will also break into groups and create concept maps, using the information you already know. You can fill in new information as the unit continues.

K What I Know	W What I Want to Know	L What I Learned

Ancient Egypt Concept Map

Name _____ Date_____

Fill in the concept map based on what you already know about Ancient Egypt. You may add extra boxes if you want to. Work with a partner to fill in additional information from the K-W-L Plus worksheet. On the next page explain the relationships among the main concept and the other ideas and concepts you have added to the web.

Ancient Egypt

Ancient Egypt Conceptual Relationships

Name _____ Date_____

Use this page to explain the relationships among the main concept, Ancient Egypt, and the other ideas, people, places, and events you have added to your concept web. Be sure to make the connection and the integration clear so that as you add more information you do not become confused.

My ideas are connected to the main concept of Ancient Egypt in the following ways:

_____

_____

_____

_____

_____

_____

_____

_____

_____

_____

_____

_____

_____

_____

_____

_____

_____

Map of Ancient Egypt

In preparation for the text selections about Ancient Egypt, it is important to know the geographical locations of the ancient cities. On the map, locate and label the following regions, cities, and bodies of water of Ancient Egypt. Make a map key to show what the colors and symbols represent on your maps.

Regions

- Upper Egypt
- Lower Egypt
- Nubia
- Valley of the Kings
- Nile Delta

Cities

- Cairo
- Heliopolis
- Giza
- Memphis
- Akhetaton (Tell el Amarna)
- Abydos
- Thebes
- Luxor
- Aswan

Bodies of Water

- Mediterranean Sea
- Red Sea
- Nile River

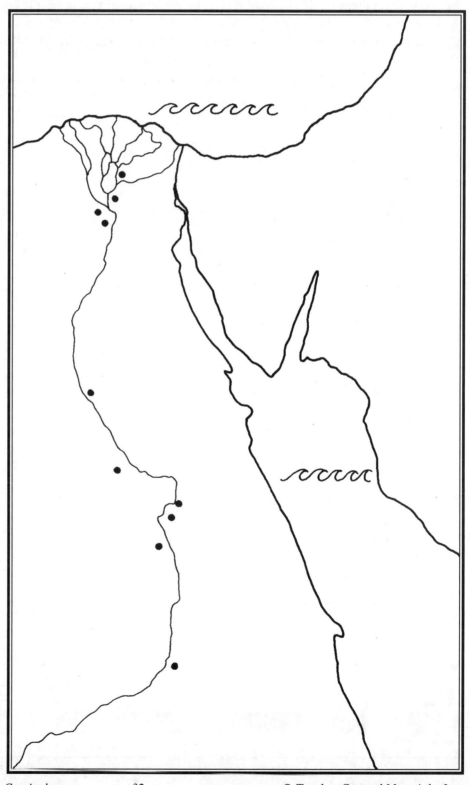

Semantic Feature Analysis

Name _____ Date_____

Use the chart below about the ancient cities of Egypt to create a semantic feature analysis. The cities are listed vertically on the left. Write characteristics of the cities on the top horizontal row. Fill in the grid, matching the city with the characteristic, marking a positive sign (+) for those features that match and a negative sign (–) for the features that do not match. Add the descriptions and explanations in the appropriate boxes.

Cities			
Cairo			
Heliopolis			
Giza			
Memphis			
Akhetaton (Tell el Amarna)			
Abydos			
Thebes			
Luxor			
Aswan			

"Saba the Farmer": Question-Answer Relationships

Narrators 1–10   **Saba,** the farmer   **Mara,** his wife   **Setu,** his friend

Nebu, his son   **Hada,** his friend   **Tika,** his daughter   **Ptah,** a peasant

Narrator 1: Ancient Egyptian life centered around the life-giving waters of the **Nile**, the longest river in the world. Many other African rivers and marshlands feed into it on its 4,150-mile journey northward to the **Mediterranean Sea.** As the river approaches the sea, it comes to a head, where it divides into many small channels and streams that form a triangle of marshy land called a **delta.**

Narrator 2: In ancient times, the delta contained seven mouths, or flows, that emptied into the sea. Today there are two main mouths—the Rosetta on the west and the Demietta on the east. **Cairo,** the capital city of modern Egypt, sits at the head of the delta. Listen now, as we go back in time to Ancient Egypt to hear the story of one farmer who lives and works along the banks of this great river.

Saba: Hello. My name is Saba, and I am a humble farmer who works the land to provide for my family. I live in a small village north of Thebes, the capital of Egypt. My village is very near the Nile in the area known as the **fertile valley.** All of us who live in Egypt, from the poorest peasant to our wealthy king, the pharaoh, depend upon the Nile. My friends Setu and Hada will help explain why the river is so important to us.

Setu: If you look at a map of Egypt, you can see that most of the land is desert. The Arabian Desert to the east and the Libyan Desert to the west are both part of the Sahara, a vast desert that covers much of northern Africa. Few people live in these desert regions because crops will not grow. Indeed, the only land with soil able to grow crops lies along the banks of the Nile. This narrow strip of land is what Saba referred to as the fertile valley.

Hada: The fertile valley replenishes its rich soil each year when the Nile floods. We consider the flooding an annual miracle. Without it, we would be unable to farm, for the land would be barren desert like the rest of Egypt. In gratitude we worship H'apy, the god of the Nile, who provides us with food and is the creator of all good.

Saba: Some years there are "high Niles." During these years, crops grow well and there is plenty to eat. In other years, the flood waters are low. The fields are baked by the sun, dry out, and are worthless for planting. If several years of low water occur in a row, we cannot grow enough food, and people starve.

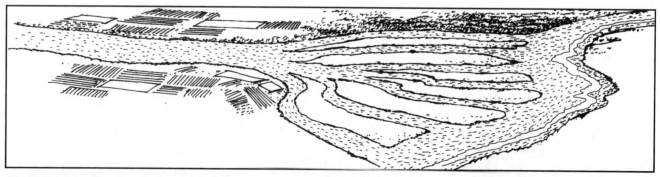

"Saba the Farmer": Question-Answer Relationships *(cont.)*

Setu: When Egypt was suffering through seven years of famine because of low flooding, King Zoser from the Old Kingdom turned to his advisor Imhotep for help. Imhotep said they needed to learn the name of the Nile god who controlled the floodgates so they could ask him to send more water to Egypt. It was believed that the god of the Nile slept in two caverns below a temple at the southern tip of Egypt. Then the Nile god, H'apy, came to King Zoser in a dream and said he would flood the land if the people would worship him. King Zoser made it so, and a high Nile ended the famine. Later, Imhotep furthers the fame of King Zoser by building the first pyramid in Egypt for him.

Narrator 3: Egypt gets almost no rain. The myth of King Zoser was a way for people to feel they could influence their fate. We now know that the right weather conditions must occur in other parts of Africa for the Nile to flow and flood. At the end of winter, snow on the mountains of central Africa melts and runs into the small tributaries that feed the Nile. Spring rains are followed by summer monsoons, swelling the Nile and its tributaries. Join us as we walk through the farmlands before the flooding begins in early August.

Nebu: Hello, Father and friends! I am working hard to finish the harvest and repair the farming equipment and irrigation canals. As you know, we cannot predict when the flooding will begin. I am hoping the yearly inundation will not be too little or too great. If the waters do not rise high enough, some farmland will remain barren. If the flooding is too great, our **irrigation system**, our home, and other buildings may be damaged.

Saba: We were fortunate to have a high Nile last year, and our crops were bountiful, as you can see. The floodwaters carried great amounts of alluvium, or silt, which greatly enriched our soil when the flooding receded. We can only hope it is the same this year. We will keep an eye on the Nilometer.

Narrator 4: A **Nilometer** is a measuring device used to help predict the height of the coming flood waters. Notches are made along the stone walls of the Nile channels to mark previous flood levels. Priests read the water level at the beginning of the year and compare it to an average year. This comparison allows people along the banks to decide whether or not they need to move their houses and livestock to higher ground and to better prepare for the planting season.

Nebu: Father, your workers are preparing the land for the flooding. Please check that they correctly dig the **channels** from the river that form our irrigation system. I will then make sure that they are cleaned out properly so water can run through them with ease. I believe Ptah is helping build an earthen **dike**.

Saba: Hello, Ptah. How is the work progressing under this hot sun?

"Saba the Farmer": Question-Answer Relationships *(cont.)*

Ptah: Greetings, Saba! The work is difficult, but if you are prepared and have a good growing season, it benefits us all. The many dikes or dams we build will hold the water when the floods start receding. They must be in good working order. It will be too late to repair or rebuild them once the inundation has begun. During the flooding, the channels are opened. They are closed once the river has reached its maximum height. The checkerboard of fields can then be drained or irrigated as needed during the rest of the year. This is a very complicated system in which every member of the village community plays a role. I am doing my part.

Narrator 5: Like Ptah, most of the men who work for Saba are peasants. However, he also has a few male slaves who help on the farm and some female slaves who work in his house with his wife. They are treated well in exchange for hard work, loyalty, and honesty. Slaves who have worked diligently for a long time are sometimes given their freedom.

Saba: Let us go to my house. I believe Mara is working with the slaves to weave some of the **flax** from the harvest. Tika is also there, sorting the grains to preserve seeds for planting and to store those we will use for food.

Narrator 6: Saba and his friends head toward his house, a structure of sun-dried bricks. The walled courtyard contains silos of grain. They pass some herds of animals and enter the courtyard where Tika is sorting grains at the silos. Geese and goats roam freely and eat grain that slaves provide. On the upper deck under a thatched roof, Mara weaves on a loom. She comes down to greet her husband and guests and sends a slave girl for refreshments.

Mara: Greetings, husband and honored guests. How are things in the fields?

Saba: It is hot and laborious work preparing for the inundation. But we had a bountiful harvest.

Mara: Yes. We grew a variety of crops this year. Wheat and barley are being ground to make the bread and beer you enjoy with your meals. The flax harvest was abundant. Even after discarding the older plants whose fibers were too tough to weave, we had plenty of young plants to provide us supple fibers for cloth and sitting mats. We will soon make ropes and heavier fabric to use in the fields.

"Saba the Farmer": Question-Answer Relationships *(cont.)*

Saba: Ah, here are the refreshments. Tika, come join us. Mara, send someone to fetch Nebu. It isn't often we have guests in the middle of the day.

Setu: I understand you also have a garden near your home.

Mara: Yes. Our house has been built far enough away from the river to be out of reach of the flooding, but irrigation channels have been dug so that there is a supply of water to the house and garden. We grow different fruits and vegetables in the garden, and I am especially proud of our vineyard. Most of the grapes are used for making wine, although we pick some for the table. You are eating some that have been dried into raisins. We also grew the figs and dates you are enjoying.

Tika: It is so pleasant sitting here overlooking the fields. Every season brings something new and exciting. I like the way we divide the seasons so that they are not based on climate but on the flooding of the Nile.

Narrator 7: The Ancient Egyptian year begins in June, and there are three seasons. The first season is known as **shait,** or **the season of inundation**. From the middle of July through October, the waters of the Nile rise, bringing with them the precious silt that makes the soil fertile.

Tika: Shait is my favorite time of the year. There is not much work on the farm when our fields are flooded. I like to go to the banks of the Nile and watch as the farmers float across the swollen river blocks of limestone to use for pyramids for the pharaoh. It seems like hard and dangerous work.

Saba: I, too, enjoy the season of inundation and look forward to the months ahead. During these months I travel by boat to check my fields and arrange other work. Sometimes the tops of the dikes remind me of a well-traveled roadway running through the water and leading me to a new adventure in trading, bartering, and meeting new people. I may even be commissioned to help with one of the pharaoh's special building projects.

Nebu: I prefer the time of the year when the water starts to recede. During **piruit, the season of emergence**, the soil is ready for planting. This brings much work but also many new possibilities. The channels will be filled with water, and we will plant a new series of crops.

"Saba the Farmer": Question-Answer Relationships *(cont.)*

Narrator 8: The planting is not easy work. First, the soil must be broken up. They use a plow called a mattock. The soil can be very heavy after the flooding, and the plowman must be strong to keep the blade down as it cuts. Then the farmers scatter barley or wheat seeds over the field, and they are plowed under. Finally, a herd of goats or sheep will be driven over the field so that their hooves can firmly embed the seed into the ground.

Nebu: Once the crops are sown, we move on to land farther away from the river. This is the first soil to dry out, and so we must make sure that the channels and ditches that carry water to this land later in the year are clear of any debris, such as trees or branches.

Narrator 9: Sometimes farmers use a **shaduf** to raise the water over the Nile's bank to the higher level of the channels. A shaduf is a type of lever made from a pole on a pivot. There is a clay weight on one end that balances a bucket on the other end. It makes it easier for farmers to collect water from the river to pour into the irrigation channels.

Nebu: From October through February we will care for our plants as they grow. This is an exciting time of the year when we see whether new irrigation and planting techniques have been successful.

Hada: Nebu will make a fine proprietor of your lands, Saba, once the great gods carry your body off to the afterworld. Although there is great satisfaction in watching crops grow, there can also be problems. Birds and insects are a continual hazard. In my own fields I often have small boys make noises to frighten the winged beasts away. Sometimes we try to catch birds with a flaxen net. We then kill them for food. Insects are a different matter. What can you do?

Setu: Nebu and Tika were too young to remember the devastation caused by the plague of **locusts**. The whole sky was blackened by the insects, and they ate everything in their path.

Saba: And storms and gales can also damage a crop beyond repair. However, despite all of these difficulties, it is rare that my land doesn't provide more than enough for my family to eat—and even provide a surplus that I can sell. The land of Egypt truly is the gift of the Nile.

Hada: That is why I like **shemu, the season of harvest**, when the crops are gathered by all members of the family and great feasts are planned. Watching the ripe grain being cut by the reapers swinging their curved wooden sickles with flint teeth is almost like watching a dance.

"Saba the Farmer": Question-Answer Relationships *(cont.)*

Narrator 10: Harvested grain is taken to the threshing floor where oxen trample the stalks, leaving chaff and grain that workers will winnow, using wooden trays. As the workers throw the grain and chaff into the air, the chaff blows away and leaves the precious grain behind. Donkeys carry it to the granaries and family silos. From February until the end of May, farmers are busy harvesting and selling their wares. This is the time of the year when the Nile is at its lowest.

Saba: Yes, and the time for getting another visit from the tax assessors, eh? I always make sure that my land is well marked with clear boundaries. This is an urgent task once the flooding has receded. Later the tax assessors will come to estimate the yield of my crop so they can calculate the taxes that have to be paid. Then, during the harvest, they return to collect my tax payment. Many is the time that I have seen disputes as landowners argued over the boundary or title of the land once the tax assessor arrived. Sometimes I pity the assessors, for they are often harassed and their lives made difficult. No one likes to give away part of the crops as a tax payment.

Mara: I feel truly thankful for all of the gifts the Nile brings to our family. Not only does it provide rich soil for growing crops but it also gives us fish and fowl for our table. The Nile nurtures **papyrus**, the long, thin reed that grows wild along the riverbanks. Saba and Nebu use it to build boats. I use papyrus to make baskets, sandals, and lightweight paper. How fortunate Egypt is to be the sole provider of this valuable and sought-after writing medium.

Tika: And don't forget how useful the Nile is for transportation and trading. The Nile is Egypt's main highway. In six places cataracts have been built to fill the river full of rocks. This creates ports for trade since it slows down the boats and makes it difficult for them to travel.

Saba: Yes, and the Nile also provides us transportation to the afterworld. During the funeral processions to the Valley of the Kings, the deceased and his possessions are floated across the Nile to be buried in a secret tomb. It is truly amazing, the number of ways our lives depend upon and benefit from this marvelous river.

"Saba the Farmer": Question-Answer Relationships *(cont.)*

Use the following QAR chart to reinforce this strategy with the students.

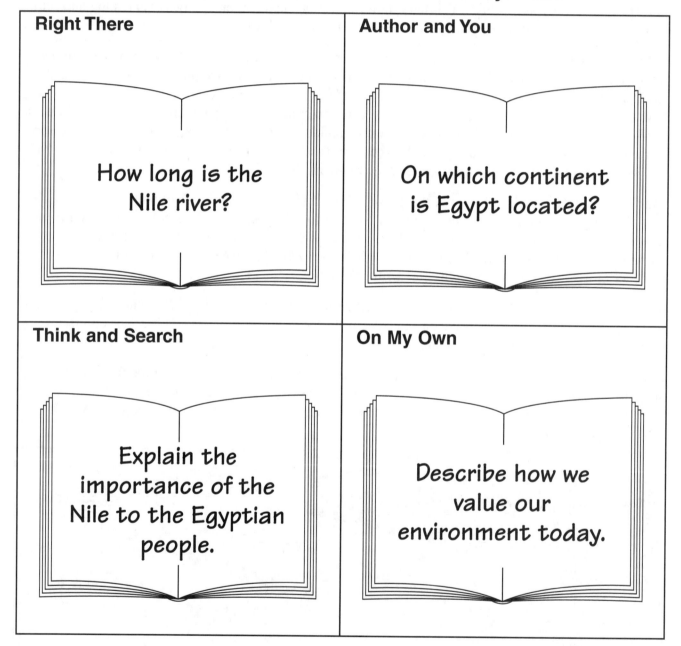

In the Book

In My Head

Right There

How long is the Nile river?

Author and You

On which continent is Egypt located?

Think and Search

Explain the importance of the Nile to the Egyptian people.

On My Own

Describe how we value our environment today.

Have students read the next selection, "Farming the Land," and complete the QAR on page 42. Have students add this page to their learning logs. Ask students to share their answers and decisions in a whole-class discussion.

Farming the Land

Directions: Read the following selection and complete page 42.

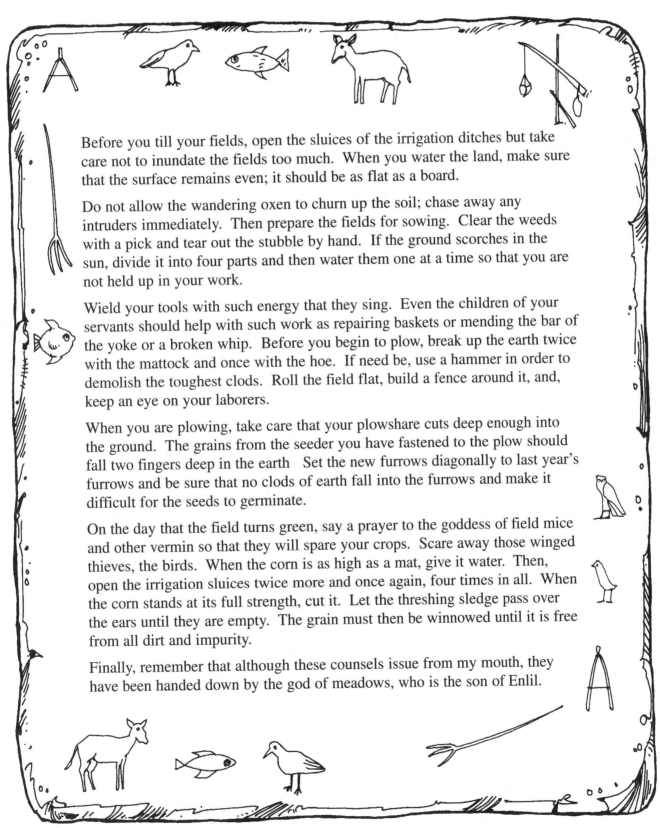

Before you till your fields, open the sluices of the irrigation ditches but take care not to inundate the fields too much. When you water the land, make sure that the surface remains even; it should be as flat as a board.

Do not allow the wandering oxen to churn up the soil; chase away any intruders immediately. Then prepare the fields for sowing. Clear the weeds with a pick and tear out the stubble by hand. If the ground scorches in the sun, divide it into four parts and then water them one at a time so that you are not held up in your work.

Wield your tools with such energy that they sing. Even the children of your servants should help with such work as repairing baskets or mending the bar of the yoke or a broken whip. Before you begin to plow, break up the earth twice with the mattock and once with the hoe. If need be, use a hammer in order to demolish the toughest clods. Roll the field flat, build a fence around it, and, keep an eye on your laborers.

When you are plowing, take care that your plowshare cuts deep enough into the ground. The grains from the seeder you have fastened to the plow should fall two fingers deep in the earth   Set the new furrows diagonally to last year's furrows and be sure that no clods of earth fall into the furrows and make it difficult for the seeds to germinate.

On the day that the field turns green, say a prayer to the goddess of field mice and other vermin so that they will spare your crops. Scare away those winged thieves, the birds. When the corn is as high as a mat, give it water. Then, open the irrigation sluices twice more and once again, four times in all. When the corn stands at its full strength, cut it. Let the threshing sledge pass over the ears until they are empty. The grain must then be winnowed until it is free from all dirt and impurity.

Finally, remember that although these counsels issue from my mouth, they have been handed down by the god of meadows, who is the son of Enlil.

"Farming the Land": Learning Log

Name _____ Date_____

Question-Answer Relationships

Title of text selection _____

In-the-Book QARs

_____

_____

_____

_____

In-My-Head QARs

_____

_____

_____

_____

_____

_____

_____

_____

Concept Web

Name _____ Date_____

Complete the concept web about farming, based on the information found in the two reading passages, "Saba the Farmer" and "Farming the Land." Be sure to include all of the concepts and ideas important to this ritual. The web has been started for you.

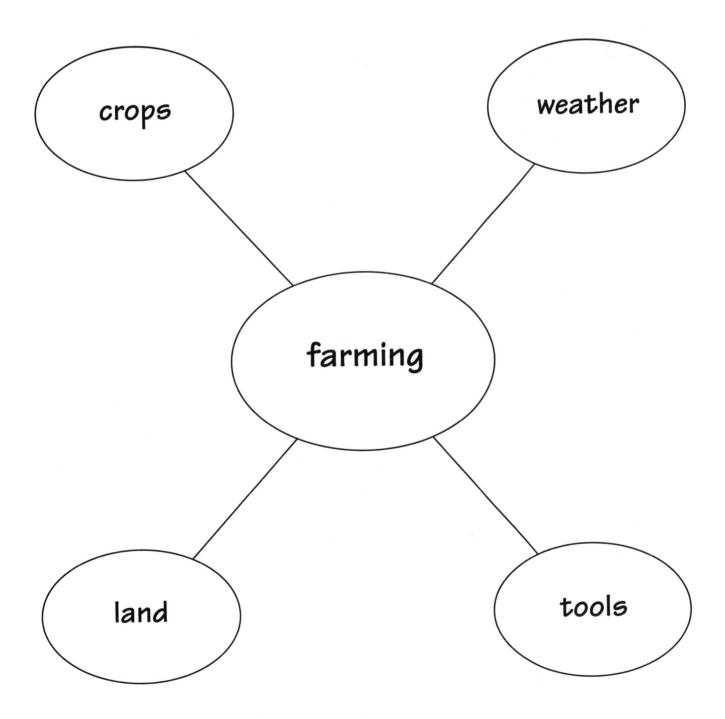

Vocabulary Self-Collection Strategy

In pairs or small groups, have students nominate one or two words or terms that they believe the class should learn or know more about. The teacher also nominates one or two words. Have students keep a vocabulary log of new words they learn throughout the Ancient Civilizations/Egypt unit. The following words can be used to initiate the vocabulary self-collection process.

delta	Nile	shait	piruit
papyrus	shaduf	locusts	shemu
flax	fertile valley	irrigation system	sluices
inundate	winnowed	Mediterranean Sea	Nilometer

Egyptian Farming

The following prompts will guide students in their reading response groups in the discussion of how the Egyptians lived off of the land. Students can read "Saba the Farmer" and "Farming the Land" and discuss the qualities of farmers and the ingenuity of the Egyptians. Students can share group responses with the whole class after they have had time to meet in small groups.

How does a flood or a drought affect all aspects of Egyptian life? Explain why the Nile floods.

Before the Egyptians used a calendar, how did they divide the year? How is it different from the way we divide the year?

What kinds of tools did the Egyptians use for farming or irrigation?

How does an Egyptian irrigation system work?

What was the significance of papyrus?

Discuss some of the crop dangers that worried the Egyptians.

Who were the gods and goddesses who guided the farmers?

Ancient Egyptian Word Sleuths

Name _____ Date_____

Imagine you are a word sleuth investigating the origins and meanings of words, terms, phrases, word families, and concepts. Collect the words from the various text selections about Ancient Egypt to include in your own archaeological research. Record your words and investigative findings in your vocabulary log or your learning log. Be sure to look for words borrowed from other languages and cultures.

Word	Origin	Meaning

Egyptian Math and Medicine

Many written and pictorial discoveries tell us that the Egyptians were very advanced in their scientific knowledge of math, astronomy, and medicine. Along with hieroglyphics for words, the Egyptians developed a symbol system for writing numbers, including fractions. There were seven basic signs for numbers, each representing a place value from one to one million. Although this system was superior to making tally marks, writing large numbers was still slow business.

There was no concept of zero and no multiplication or division. Instead, the Egyptians added the number to itself as many times as needed for multiplication or subtracted repeatedly to divide. Many papyrus scrolls exist that are filled with mathematics problems involving everyday situations. They include examples of how to divide rations among workers, how to calculate the area of a field, and even how to calculate the area of a circle. Keeping accurate records and computations was important to all Egyptian farmers, merchants, tradesmen, and scribes.

Egyptians also made advances by using astronomy. From their study of the heavens and their sense of arithmetic, the Egyptians were able to measure time and develop an extremely accurate calendar. They divided the 24 hours of day and night into equal segments, 12 hours measured from sunrise to sunset and 12 hours from sunset to sunrise.

In addition to the 24-hour day, we can also attribute our yearly calendar to the Egyptians. The Babylonians had developed a lunar calendar based on the phases of the moon. The Egyptians based their farmers' calendar on both the moon and the star Sirius. They had observed that Sirius, the brightest star in the sky, appeared at the same time each year, and this corresponded to the time of the year that the Nile flooded. This calendar was more accurate than the lunar calendar because it corresponded almost exactly to their seasons.

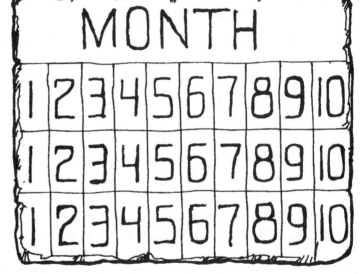

Egyptians also developed a "civil" calendar of 365 days, in which the year was divided into 12 months, each with three 10-day weeks, or 30 days. There were four months in each of the three annual Egyptian seasons. The five days left over were used as holy festival days at the end of the year. Because the Egyptians did not provide for a leap year, the civil calendar became more and more out of step with the farmers' calendar as time passed.

Other discoveries show the Egyptians to be highly skilled doctors and surgeons. Papyrus medical texts tell us that the Egyptians believed the heart had vital control throughout the body and that it "spoke" through the pulse. They knew the heart circulated blood, but they also believed it distributed air, water, nerves, and food to the body. They regarded the brain as being of little or no consequence to the functions of the body. In fact, the brain was so unimportant to Egyptians that it was discarded during the mummification process. Other organs were preserved in containers called canopic jars, which were buried with the dead.

Egyptian Math and Medicine *(cont.)*

Ancient medical writings are divided into sections listing medicines and giving advice to doctors on how to treat such ailments as burns, head injuries, tumors, eye diseases, and stomach problems. The writings stress the importance of careful observation and gentle treatment, including rest and soothing herbal remedies. One treatment recommends wrapping a slice of raw meat over a wound. After a day, the patient removes the meat and applies grease, honey, and lint until the wound heals. Willow leaves, which contain salicylic acid, or aspirin, were applied to wounds to reduce inflammation. Copper and sodium salts were applied to help dry a wound. Cream and flour were mixed to make a cast for a broken limb. Faced with more difficult diseases for which they did not understand the causes, doctors might mix potions with magic spells or prayers. Then, even if the medicine failed, the patient would be comforted by the prayers.

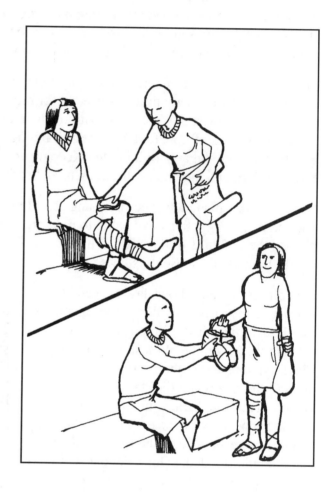

Egyptian doctors were trained in the temple medical school. They were considered the best in the world and traveled all over the Near East to treat foreign royalty. While royalty and wealthy families had their own doctors, anyone could consult the doctors in any temple's House of Life, the Egyptian equivalent of a hospital. For a private visit, doctors were paid in goods, like any other service in Egypt. A typical fee for visiting the doctor during childbirth might include a bronze jar, a pair of sandals, some baskets, and oil.

Although we no longer use the exact calendar, mathematics, or medicine developed by the Ancient Egyptians, their attention to detail, accuracy of observations, and use of logic were remarkable for that time and have heavily influenced modern developments.

Choose one of the following activities to show your understanding of the passage:

1. Write a diary entry describing your day as a doctor in Ancient Egypt.

2. Draw and label a picture of a House of Life. Be sure to include items for treatment and payment.

3. Make an Egyptian calendar. Label the months, weeks, and days. Include the three seasons and the five festival days.

Group Mapping Activity

After reading "Egyptian Math and Medicine" have students create a map that explains what they believe to be the important concepts and ideas from the text. Students should not talk to classmates or look back at the text. Share the sample map below with students, if necessary.

1. Have students share their maps with a partner or members in a small group.

> Remind students to explain the following:
> - what they chose to include
> - how they chose to design their maps
> - why they made their specific choices

2. Have students work collaboratively with partners or in small groups to finish their maps.

3. Encourage students to review the text to clarify questions or information.

Sample Group Map for "Egyptian Math and Medicine"

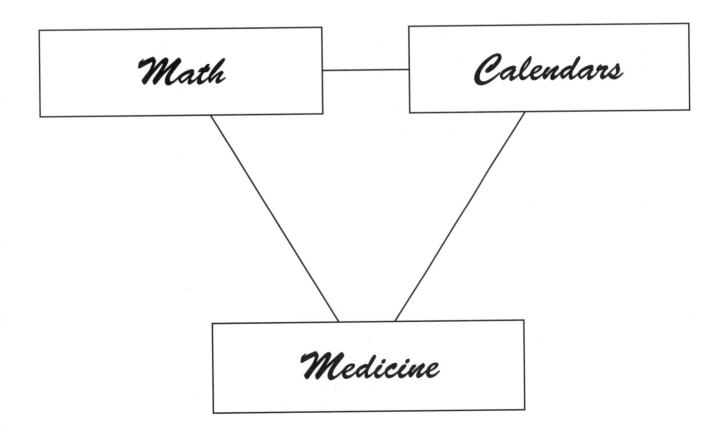

Doctor's Double-Entry Journal

Name _____ Date_____

What did the Egyptians stress when dealing with medical issues?

_____

_____

_____

_____

_____

_____

What kinds of ailments did the Egyptians suffer?

_____

_____

_____

_____

_____

_____

What can we learn about ancient Egyptian medical practices?

_____

_____

_____

_____

_____

_____

Do any modern civilizations follow the ancient Egyptian medical treatments?

_____

_____

_____

_____

_____

_____

Building the Pyramids

Narrators 1–12   **Imhotep,** the vizier   **Factah,** the foreman

Sadah, the stonemason   **King Khufu** (Cheops)   **Asashti,** the architect

King Zoser   **King Menes**   **King Khafre**

Cabal, the surveyor   **King Tutankhamen** (Tut)

Wasat, the engineer

Narrator 1: The Egyptians were an advanced civilization of people highly knowledgeable in math, science, and the arts. Some of their most astounding skills can be seen in their magnificent architecture. Their most famous buildings include royal palaces, vast temples, and, of course, the pyramids. These stone giants were not conceived overnight. Many stages and years transpired before the first pyramid was ever built. Join us now for a walk through time as we visit some leaders and builders of Ancient Egypt. We begin with the first pharaoh of unified Egypt, King Menes.

Menes: We Egyptians go to a great deal of trouble to see that we pass on to the next world as easily as possible. One of the most important aspects leading to a happy afterlife is the tomb we are buried in. This is especially true for the pharaoh, or king, since he is also regarded as a living god. Egyptians believe that when the pharaoh dies, he joins the immortal gods. Some believe that his spirit, or ba, flies to the horizon in the shape of the hawk god Horus to be joined with the sun. Others believe his spirit joins those of his ancestors as a star in the sky or descends into the Underworld to rule as the god Osiris. Therefore, we believe that if we can keep his body safe for all eternity, his ba will be able to return to it, and his power will preserve Egypt.

Narrator 2: Starting with the first dynasty during the Archaic Period, the pharaoh, King Menes, was buried in a tomb called a **mastaba**, which in Arabic means bench. The mastaba was like a house with rooms. Later mastabas became grand structures containing a chapel and other rooms for ceremonies. The development of building these grand tombs for the pharaoh was taken a step further by King Zoser during the Old Kingdom—the age of the pyramids.

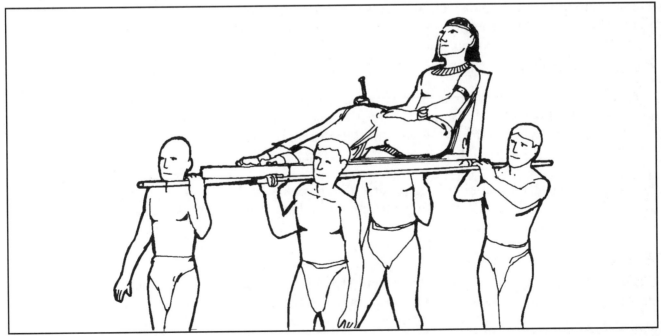

Building the Pyramids *(cont.)*

Zoser: Welcome to my land! I am the pharaoh of all Egypt. Now that I have come to the throne, I have decided that I shall be buried in a grand tomb that will last forever. Previous tombs, like the mastaba for King Menes, were made of mud bricks that crumble over time. To keep my ba content, I will be preserved in stone in a new manner befitting my status. For this, I call on my vizier, Imhotep.

Narrator 3: Imhotep was a man of great intellect and courage. Besides being the king's chief architect, he also held the revered status of chief sculptor and chief carpenter. He was an astronomer, doctor, and advisor in the ways of the gods. Because of his great knowledge and talents, he had reached the second-highest office in the land—vizier to the pharaoh.

Imhotep: I hold my position of great power as an honor. Being the vizier is much like being a prime minister or president. I am a friend to the pharaoh and consult with him on matters of government, religion, and the people. I accepted the building of King Zoser's tomb as a privilege and will design the greatest tomb the world has ever seen.

One way to accomplish this feat is to build upwards. The base will remain a mastaba, a complex of temples and other rooms. However, for the remainder of the tomb I have something more ambitious in mind. I will build five more mastabas, one on top of the other, with each succeeding mastaba being slightly smaller than the one beneath it. The six steps will reach a height of nearly 2,000 feet. I call my new style of tomb a **step pyramid**.

Narrator 4: No one knows for certain if Imhotep planned his design in advance or thought of it as the work progressed. It is also uncertain why he chose this particular shape. Some experts believe that the shape of Imhotep's step pyramid created a stairway to heaven for the pharaoh's ba. Most agree it is a very stable and strong shape, therefore having a good chance of lasting a long time. It is also a sensible shape since the majority of the stone is in the bottom half. Hence, the higher you go, the fewer stones you have to move.

Later pyramids would continue with Imhotep's basic shape but with smooth sides. This was said to represent the rays of the sun shining down on the desert and creating a pathway to the sky. Other experts believe the shape to represent the ben-ben stone, or the first sacred mound of earth, which rose out of the waters and was used by the sun god to stand upon and create the universe.

Imhotep: The entire step pyramid complex will eventually include temples, chapels, other buildings, and courtyards. Like the other burial grounds, it will be on the west bank of the Nile, where the sun sets and leaves for other worlds. Each person's ba must make the same journey. To assist, we build all of our tombs as close as possible to the spot where the sun leaves the earth.

Narrator 5: The step pyramid of King Zoser still stands today in Saqqara near the ancient capital of Memphis in northern Egypt. Although the base mastaba has crumbled, it is still an impressive sight and a tribute to early architecture. King Zoser began an age of pyramid building that would last for over 600 years. Pyramid building reached its height during the Old Kingdom period. More than 80 pyramids still exist today, reminders of the ingenuity and perseverance of these ancient people. King Khufu also decided to build a pyramid that would be bigger, better, and more magnificent than anything built before. We join him now during the reign of the Fourth Dynasty, about 2573 B.C.

Building the Pyramids *(cont.)*

Khufu: My father, King Sneferu, built the first pyramid with smooth sides. It is in the desert at Dahshur, a few miles south of Saqqara. I will build my tomb at **Giza**, a few miles north of Saqqara. My pyramid will be so grand as to be truly worthy of my greatness and power. The plans for my Great Pyramid show it will cover 13 acres. Thousands of laborers will be needed, along with skilled craftsmen, stonemasons, carpenters, surveyors, foremen, engineers, and overseers to make sure everything is done correctly and the results are magnificent beyond anything anyone has seen before.

Cabal: I am the chief surveyor for the king. My tasks require knowledge of geometry and astronomy. Our first step in building the Great Pyramid is to select a proper site on which to build. It must be on the west bank of the Nile and above flood level but close enough to the water so that the huge building stones can be transported by ship from the limestone quarries across the Nile and then moved by sleds to the building site.

To begin, we need a solid foundation. All of the sand, gravel, and loose rock must be removed until the solid rock floor of the desert lays bare. It is also very important that the four sides of the pyramid face exactly in the four directions—north, south, east, and west. To do this we build a circular wall on the rock base. At night, I mark the place on the wall where a star rises in the sky. After the star sets, I draw another line on the wall. I then draw a line from both of my marks to the center of the circle. By bisecting this angle, I will be able to find true north. The foundation must also be perfectly level. I call on Wasat for this bit of engineering.

Wasat: When any sort of container is filled with water, the surface of the water is level. We use this principle on a huge scale. Once the four sides of the base have been marked out, we dig a vast network of trenches that crisscross the marked area. The trenches are then filled with water, and the water naturally finds its own level. The water line is marked, the water is drained from the trenches, and the land is excavated to the water lines. We end up with a perfectly level site. I am very proud of the work that we do, for this is by far the largest site ever to be leveled. Now we are ready to square and measure the sides.

Narrator 6: How accurate were the ancient Egyptians at measuring and leveling? The base of King Khufu's Great Pyramid was off level by only five-eighths of an inch between the southeast and northwest corners.

Cabal: Once again I am needed to make sure the base is a perfect square. This is done using measuring cords made from flax fibers. We take a length of cord and divide it into 12 equal units. A knot is made at the third unit, the seventh unit, and at the end. The cord is then formed into a perfect right triangle and fitted into the corners. The length of each side can also be measured using these cords.

Narrator 6: The Egyptians' use of geometry was astounding. Although flax stretched when it was used, the difference between the longest and shortest sides of the Great Pyramid was only 7.9 inches. Considering each side is more than 750 feet long, the error is remarkably small. Many experts believe that such accuracy could only have been achieved by the use of astronomy as well.

Building the Pyramids *(cont.)*

Sadah: While the site is being prepared and marked, I am hard at work at the limestone quarries, overseeing the cutting of the slabs. I am only one of hundreds of stonemasons working on the Great Pyramid. The only tools we use are metal chisels and saws and wooden mallets, hammers, and wedges.

My first task is to outline carefully on the slab where it will be cut. Then, using the mallet and chisel, I punch a number of cracks along the outline. Next, I drive wooden wedges into the cracks and soak them with water. The wedges absorb the water and expand, thus splitting the slab. We then lift the huge slabs with wooden levers, using a rock as a pivot, or fulcrum. With these simple tools and methods, we stonemasons will cut over 2,300,000 blocks of limestone, some weighing as much as 33,000 pounds!

Factah: As chief foreman, I have the responsibility of seeing that the slabs of limestone are placed exactly where the architects want them. The inside of the pyramid is made from limestone quarried in Giza, but the better-quality limestone for the outside comes from Tura, on the east bank. These blocks are put on logs and rolled to the edge of the Nile. There they are loaded onto barges and rowed down the river. This is done when the Nile is at its highest, during the inundation. During this time the Nile is only one quarter mile from the pyramid building site. Once at Giza, the blocks are mounted on sleds and dragged into place along ramps, or inclined planes, that encircle the rising pyramid. Mud and mortar are used to help reduce the friction from the dragging sleds.

This is not an easy task. The laborers sometimes pull the slab over rollers to go up more difficult ramps. Although we try to be as careful as possible, there are still numerous accidents, and hardly a day goes by without some of the laborers being killed or injured. Eventually, one by one, the slabs are put into place.

Building the Pyramids *(cont.)*

Khufu: Many people believe that my pyramids are built by slaves, but that is only partly true. In addition to these workers, peasant farmers help out for three or four months every year when the Nile floods their fields. They are paid for their services with food, oil, and cloth. The farmers hope that by helping with my preparation for death, they will please the gods and be rewarded in the next world.

Factah: I have the greatest admiration for the architects. Most of the blocks fit together so well that no mortar is needed to hold them in place. Some of the joints between the slabs are so tight you can't even slide the blade of a knife between them.

Sadah: The very last stone to be put into place is called the capstone. Its sides slope to end in a common point. The very top level of the pyramid has a hole. A plug is carved on the underside of the capstone. This plug fits into the hole and holds the capstone in place. When it is time for the capstone to be fitted, there is great rejoicing, for we know that the pyramid is almost finished. The sides of the great pyramid will be smoothed and polished. The stonemasons will work downwards from the top, removing the dirt ramps as they work toward the base. Finally, the work is complete. The pharaoh has his pathway to the gods, and we all believe that the fruits of our labor will last forever.

Narrator 7: **King Khufu's Great Pyramid of Giza** is one of the Seven Wonders of the Ancient World. It stands 481 feet high, about the height of a 40-story building. It is reported that over 10,000 laborers worked every day for over 20 years to complete it. If you view the pyramid from the outside, it appears to be solid stone. But inside are many tunnels and rooms used for the burial.

Asashti: I am the king's chief architect. I work out the details for the tunnels and **burial chambers**. The interior contains three burial chambers, each intended at one time to be the final resting place for the king. One chamber, mistakenly called the Queen's Chamber, was never intended for Khufu's wife, who was, in fact, buried outside the Great Pyramid. King Khufu's burial chamber, unlike many other kings' burial chambers, is inside the pyramid itself and not hidden underground.

Originally planned on a much smaller scale, Khufu's pyramid was enlarged as the king's reign was prolonged, until the final burial chamber was established in the midsection of the pyramid at the end of a steeply ascending Grand Gallery. It is here in the burial chamber that the **sarcophagus**, or stone coffin containing the king's body, will lie. The chamber walls are carved with descriptions of the changes that the king will go through until he becomes a god. It also contains false doors and openings to the outer world through which the king's ba can pass.

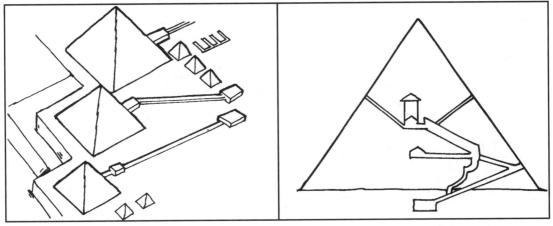

Building the Pyramids *(cont.)*

Narrator 8: The Grand Gallery contains the most treasured possessions of the pharaoh for him to use in the afterlife. To prevent violation of the royal tomb, the passage leading to the Grand Gallery is sealed by plug stones. Workers slide the plug stones into place and make their way to the exit through an **escape shaft.** However, even the most secretive and complex plans can't deter thieves, and the Great Pyramid failed to give the pharaoh's mummy the protection intended. Many treasures and large quantities of gold were buried with each pharaoh. With so many people working on one phase of the pyramid or another, it was difficult to ensure security for such sought-after riches. In addition to stealing funeral items, robbers hacked away at the mummified body to steal the jewelry inside the wrappings. Sometimes they even set fire to gold coffins to melt off the metal.

Khufu: Still, the pyramid is only part of my entire funeral site. There is also a temple for the mummification rituals and a roofed causeway, carved with scenes from my life, that leads to the temple at the foot of the pyramid. This is where the priests will make offerings to feed my spirit. Also, near the base of the Great Pyramid, my "solar boats" are buried. My spirit will need these to move about the many lakes and rivers in the next world. Coming from a land so dependent upon the waters of the Nile, it is only logical that our heaven will also be filled with water.

Narrator 9: King Khufu is best known today by his Greek name, Cheops. Although King Khufu as the pharaoh was worshiped as a god-king, he was also a tyrant and oppressor who forced his people to build the Great Pyramid. He was disliked and even hated. When King Khufu died, his body was carried from his palace to Giza, the site of the Great Pyramid. It was prepared for burial, and his mummified body was placed on a funeral boat and pulled by workmen to the pyramid. Khufu's son, King Khafre, had his pyramid built next to that of his father's.

Khafre: I will follow tradition and build another pyramid. But I also want to leave a lasting memorial of myself in a way that no one else has. How do I create something different from anything seen before and protect my tomb at the same time? I know—I will have the likeness of my face carved in the form of a huge statue and place it before my tomb. This Great Sphinx will scare off thieves and protect my dead body.

Narrator 10: The Great Sphinx stands about 200 feet high. It was common for a deity to be represented by a huge statue or sculpture in Egypt. Usually the statue was of a human body with an animal head. The most popular animal was a lion, and there are statues with lions' heads guarding many temples and tombs. The Great Sphinx differs in that it is so immense and its form is reversed. It has the head of a god—or, in this case, Khafre's face—and the body of a lion. The word "sphinx" may have come from the Egyptian *shesep ankh,* which means "living image" or "statue."

Building the Pyramids *(cont.)*

Narrator 11:   Not all of the kings who built the pyramids enslaved their people in the way Khufu did. The third pyramid at Giza was built by King Khafre's son-in-law, Menkaure. Here was an honest, just, and compassionate ruler greatly admired and loved by his people. Of course, not all pharaohs built pyramids for their tombs, either. Building such a large burial tomb required vast amounts of work by hundreds of workers over many years. Sometimes the pharaoh would die before his pyramid was completed, leaving the royal family in quite a predicament. They also realized that the enormous cost of building did not ensure them a sacred and untouched burial. Therefore, pharaohs ruling after the Old Kingdom began hiding their tombs in the desert cliffs near Thebes. This region eventually became known as the **Valley of the Kings**. King Tutankhamen was just one of the many pharaohs of the New Kingdom to be buried in these sacred cliffs.

Tutankhamen: The tombs cut into the rock cliffs, with their underground tunnels and passageways, are more complex than the pyramids. A well, or shaft, is sunk in the main corridor of the tomb. In addition, a false wall is built on the other side of the shaft to make it look as if the tomb has come to an end. The tombs are also protected by strict laws. When thieves are caught, they are put on trial and forced to confess how they got into the tomb. The accused are then brutally executed by being thrust upon the points of sharp stakes stuck into the ground and left to die in agony.

Narrator 12:   But the tomb thieves of Ancient Egypt were not even discouraged by this cruel form of punishment. All the royal tombs have been robbed except those of Tutankhamen at Thebes and Psusennes at Tannis. The Ancient Egyptians left so much behind for us to admire. Wonderful buildings, artifacts, art, and written texts have survived over the centuries. The most famous of these, however, are the pyramids, which truly represent some of man's greatest technological achievements and which helped make Ancient Egypt one of the great civilizations.

Beginning Researcher

Name _____ Date_____

Becoming an Architect

You are a world famous architect specializing in the structural magnificence of the Egyptian palaces, temples, and pyramids. Your research project is to study the pyramids built by the Ancient Egyptians. You want to find out what each pyramid symbolized to the Egyptian people. In your research you want to compare the pyramids to other burial tombs of other pharaohs. You have been asked to lead a tour group through the pyramids, and you want to make sure you know all of the information. You may gather architectural journal articles, photographs, or other artifacts throughout your research. You will take a one-week trip to visit the pyramids, take your own photographs, and collect authentic artifacts for further research. Keep a journal to record notes, comments, and questions that require further inquiry. Use the space below to write your beginning research ideas. Present your research findings to your class before you take the tour group to Egypt.

Phase One: The teacher reads a section of related text to the class, and you take notes and develop research ideas.

_____

_____

_____

_____

Phase Two: Make a list of appropriate sources (primary and secondary) you should read and then take notes from. Write down questions that need further investigation.

_____

_____

_____

_____

Phase Three: Initiate and carry out research (for example, visit the library or appropriate Internet sites).

_____

_____

_____

_____

Architect's Journal

Name _____ Date_____

How did the Egyptians build the pyramids, palaces, and temples?	What can we learn from the magnificent buildings built by the Egyptians?
Who designed the pyramids?	Has anyone tried to replicate the pyramids?
What materials were needed?	What materials might we use today?

Egyptian Calendar

On your trip to Egypt to study the pyramids, temples, and palaces, use an Egyptian calendar. Explain how this calendar differed from the lunar calendar and from the calendar we use today.

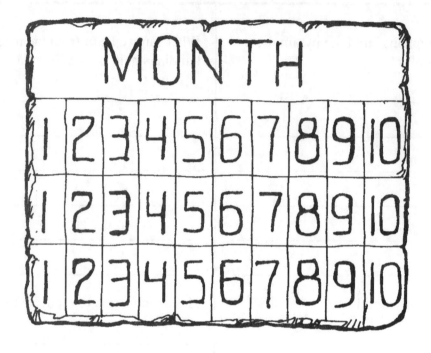

_____

_____

_____

_____

_____

_____

_____

_____

_____

_____

_____

Egyptian Buildings

Name _____ Date_____

The Egyptians were advanced in their thinking about science, math, and the arts. The magnificent architecture found in Egypt is evidence of their brilliance. The most famous buildings include royal palaces, temples, and the pyramids. Many people worked long and hard to construct such powerful structures. After reading the passage "Building the Pyramids," organize the information using the following graphs and maps.

- Create a chart or a graph depicting your estimated measurements of each pyramid, palace, and temple.

- Create a visual map of the pyramids.

- Create a semantic map explaining the relationships between the pyramids and the temples and palaces.

Analysis of Egyptian Pyramids

Name _____ Date_____

Use the semantic feature analysis below to show the relationships among the different types of tombs used in Ancient Egypt.

Egyptian Pyramid Semantic Feature Analysis

Types of Tombs	Foundation			
	gravel	sand	rock	built by slaves
Step Pyramid				
Great Pyramid of Giza				
Great Sphinx				
Valley of the Kings				

Architectural Vocabulary Log

Introduce the following words to help students start their architectural vocabulary logs. Students should write the definition for each word and use the word in a sentence or draw illustrations to help them remember the word. Encourage students to add words as they learn more about pyramid building. A generic form for vocabulary log pages is provided on page 236. You may wish to supply students with copies of this form or design a form of your own for students to add to their vocabulary logs.

pyramid   buried chamber

escape shaft   mastaba

sarcophagus   Valley of the Kings

Great Sphinx   step pyramid

Great Pyramids at Giza

Guided Writing Prompts

Directions: Use the following writing prompts to express your ideas relating to the architecture and architects of the times.

Imagine you are one of King Khufu's chief architects and the design you submit to the king is rejected. What happens to you?

Imagine you are chief foreman on the Giza pyramid project and there is a drought, causing the barges carrying the limestone to be stranded up the river.

Imagine you are King Tutankhamen. Describe your life as a pharaoh.

As an architect, you are asked to design one of the wonders of the modern world. What are your ideas for this structure?

Pyramid Building Response Groups

The following prompts will guide students in their reading response group discussions of how the Egyptians built the pyramids. Students can read the text selection "Building the Pyramids" and discuss the brilliance of the kings and their respect for burial tombs. Students can share group responses with the whole class after they have had time to meet in small groups.

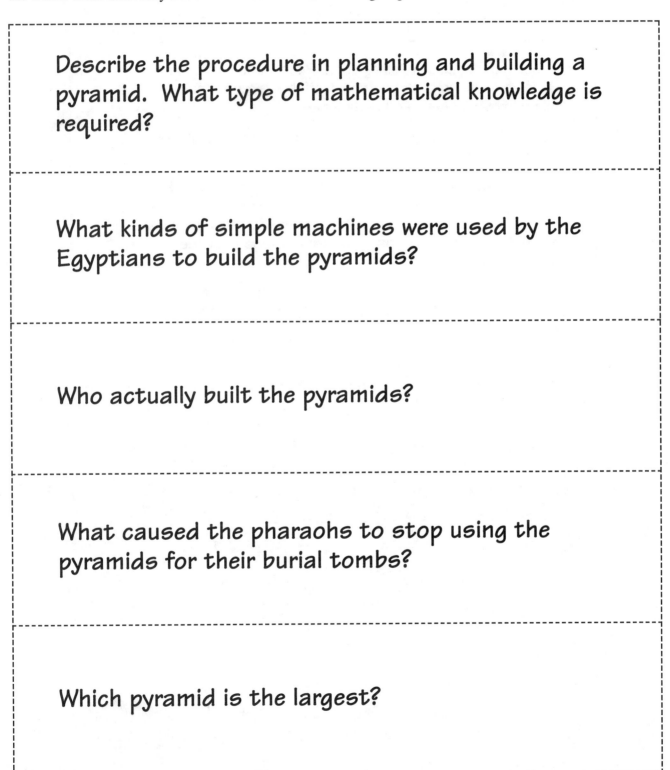

Describe the procedure in planning and building a pyramid. What type of mathematical knowledge is required?

What kinds of simple machines were used by the Egyptians to build the pyramids?

Who actually built the pyramids?

What caused the pharaohs to stop using the pyramids for their burial tombs?

Which pyramid is the largest?

Ancient Egyptian Burial Rituals

Content DRTA (Directed Reading-Thinking Activity)

Before reading, have students predict what the story will be about based on the title and the cover of the book and the students' background knowledge. Students can work with partners or in small groups to brainstorm ideas and list everything they know about Ancient Egypt in their learning logs.

- Announce the specific topic "Burial Rituals and Ceremonies." Have students go back and check off the items on their lists that relate to burial rituals and ceremonies.

- Ask students to add to their lists new ideas that directly relate to burial rituals and ceremonies.

- After students read the text selection "Beshet the Burial Priest," have them evaluate their predictions by circling the correct items they have on their lists. Students can make new predictions before they continue to read the next passage (until the new narrator speaks).

- As a whole class, discuss predictions and outcomes and specific knowledge that was learned through the text selection.

Burial Rituals and Ceremonies

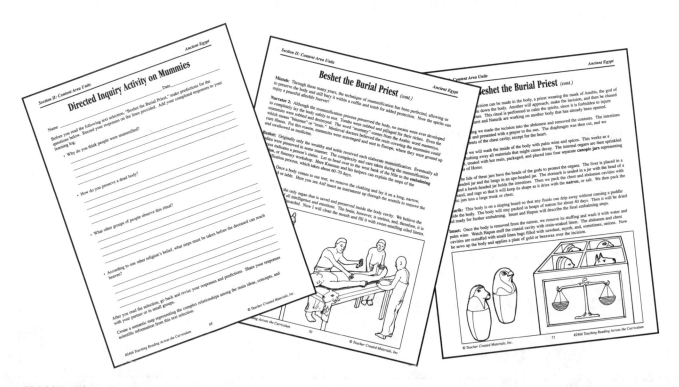

Pre-Reading Strategy

Name _____ Date_____

You will be reading a text selection, "Beshet the Burial Priest." As you read the passage, think about the following questions and suggestions, and develop thorough and complete answers. Record your answers in your learning logs.

- Create a semantic map to organize the information you already know about the mummies and the new information you learn from reading the passage.

- Add new vocabulary words from the passage to your vocabulary log.

- Choose two or three words to nominate for the class vocabulary self-collection activity.

Think about the questions. You may use the lines provided for notes or ideas to help you get started.

1. How did the Egyptians view death?

   _____

   _____

2. How would you describe the burial rites in Ancient Egypt?

   _____

   _____

3. What can we learn from the Egyptians about death and burial rites?

   _____

   _____

4. What is your opinion of mummification?

   _____

   _____

Directed Inquiry Activity on Mummies

Name _____ Date_____

Before you read the following text selection, "Beshet the Burial Priest," make predictions for the questions below. Record your responses on the lines provided. Add your completed responses to your learning log.

• Why do you think people were mummified?

_____

_____

_____

_____

• How do you preserve a dead body?

_____

_____

_____

_____

• What other groups of people observe this ritual?

_____

_____

_____

_____

• According to one other religion's belief, what steps must be taken before the deceased can reach heaven?

_____

_____

_____

_____

After you read the selection, go back and revise your responses and predictions. Share your responses with your partner or in small groups.

Create a semantic map representing the complex relationships among the main ideas, concepts, and scientific information from this text selection.

Beshet the Burial Priest

Narrators 1–5

Hapun, Haret, Naturik,

Beshet, Alexus, Mintah, the priests

Knunum, the embalmer

Imset, Damutef, Atif, Knunum's helpers

Narrator 1: Many people believe the Ancient Egyptians were preoccupied with death. However, it was their love of life that dictated the extreme care given to those who died. The practice of mummification was a symbol of the Ancient Egyptians' desire to continue living in the next world as lavishly as they lived in this one. Beshet, one of the priests overseeing burial processes, will guide us as we learn about the many steps of the burial rites in Ancient Egypt.

Beshet: I am a priest, but rather than serving a god in a temple, I am responsible for supervising the many stages of burial. It is my job to make sure that the deceased is fully equipped to make the journey into the afterlife by observing the proper customs, rituals, and **mummification** steps. The entire process is quite complex.

Mintah: We believe that when a person dies, various spirits are released from the body. The **ka** is the person's spiritual double, or shadow. The ka is formed at birth and has an independent existence. It can move freely from place to place and enjoy life with the gods in heaven. The ka needs nourishment, so we bring offerings of food and drink to the tomb for its sustenance.

Beshet: The **ba** is like the soul and symbolizes the living personality. The ba has the body of a bird because it flies out of the tomb during the day to visit its relatives and loved ones. The ba returns at night to its tomb.

Mintah: There is also the **akh**, or the supernatural power of the deceased. It is the akh that makes the perilous journey to the Underworld to be judged for the afterlife. With all of these spirits it is important that the body of the deceased be preserved so that its spirits can recognize it and return safely to it. Without its spirits, the deceased cannot exist in the afterlife. Here comes Alexus. He is a very old priest who remembers how things were done in the beginning.

Alexus: In the earliest days, a body was "put to rest" in the sleeping position with the elbows and knees drawn together. The body was placed in a pit dug into the hot sands. Items such as jars of food or tools were also placed in the pit for use in the afterlife. Sand was pushed over the body, allowing it to dry quickly and wither but not decay. However, these graves were subject to raids by hyenas and jackals, which dug up the bodies and chewed them to pieces. This would not do if the spirits were going to recognize the bodies and return. Therefore, we began protecting bodies in coffins made from reeds and wooden planks and sealed in tombs. Still, the coffins did not protect bodies from decay, and once again the spirits were left with no home.

Beshet the Burial Priest *(cont.)*

Mintah: Through these many years, the technique of mummification has been perfected, allowing us to preserve the body and still bury it within a coffin and tomb for added protection. Now the spirits can enjoy a peaceful afterlife forever!

Narrator 2: Although the mummification process preserved the body, no means were ever developed to completely lay the body safely to rest. Tombs were robbed and pillaged for their riches. Even the mummies were robbed and destroyed. The word "mummy" comes from the Arabic word *mummiya,* which means "bitumen" or "resin." Medieval doctors believed the resin covering the mummies could cure illness. For this reason, mummies were scavenged and sent to Europe, where they were ground up and swallowed as medicine.

Beshet: Originally only the wealthy and noble received such elaborate mummification. Eventually all bodies were preserved in some manner. The complexity and care taken during the mummification process indicates a person's status. Let us head over to the west bank of the Nile to the **embalming pavilion,** or funerary workshop. Here Knunum and his helpers can explain the steps of the mummification process, which takes about 60–70 days.

Knunum: Once a body comes to our tent, we remove the clothing and lay it on a long, narrow, wooden board or table. Here you see Atif insert an instrument up through the nostrils to remove the brain.

Atif: The heart is the only organ that is saved and preserved inside the body cavity. We believe the heart is the center of all intelligence and emotions. The brain, however, is useless, and, therefore, it is removed in bits and discarded. Now I will clean the mouth and fill it with sweet-smelling oiled linens.

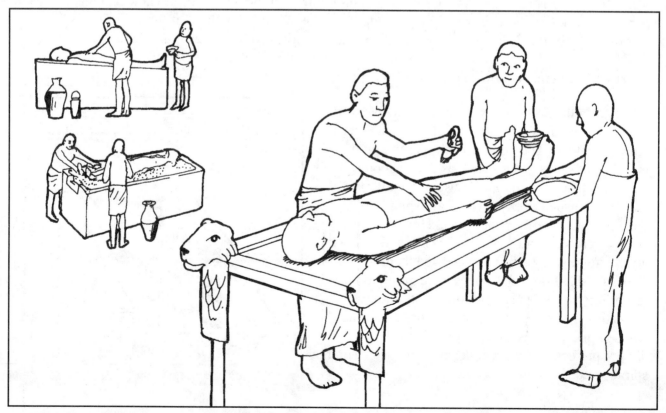

Beshet the Burial Priest *(cont.)*

Knunum: Before an incision can be made in the body, a priest wearing the mask of Anubis, the god of embalming, draws a line down the body. Another will approach, make the incision, and then be chased from the area with curses. This ritual is performed to calm the spirits, since it is forbidden to injure another Egyptian. Haret and Naturik are working on another body that has already been opened.

Haret: This morning we made the incision into the abdomen and removed the contents. The intestines were put into a jar and presented with a prayer to the sun. The diaphragm was then cut, and we removed the contents of the chest cavity, except for the heart.

Naturik: Now we will wash the inside of the body with palm wine and spices. This works as a disinfectant, flushing away all materials that might cause decay. The internal organs are then sprinkled with perfume, treated with hot resin, packaged, and placed into four separate **canopic jars** representing the four sons of Horus.

Haret: The lids of these jars have the heads of the gods to protect the organs. The liver is placed in a human-headed jar and the lungs in an ape-headed jar. The stomach is sealed in a jar with the head of a jackal, and a hawk-headed jar holds the intestines. Then we pack the chest and abdomen cavities with straw, sand, and rags so that it will keep its shape as it dries with the **natron**, or salt. We then pack the canopic jars into a large trunk or chest.

Naturik: This body is on a sloping board so that any fluids can drip away without causing a puddle inside the body. The body will stay packed in heaps of natron for about 40 days. Then it will be dried and ready for further embalming. Imset and Hapun will describe the final embalming steps.

Imset: Once the body is removed from the natron, we remove its stuffing and wash it with water and palm wine. Watch Hapun stuff the cranial cavity with resin-soaked linen. The abdomen and chest cavities are restuffed with small linen bags filled with sawdust, myrrh, and, sometimes, onions. Now he sews up the body and applies a plate of gold or beeswax over the incision.

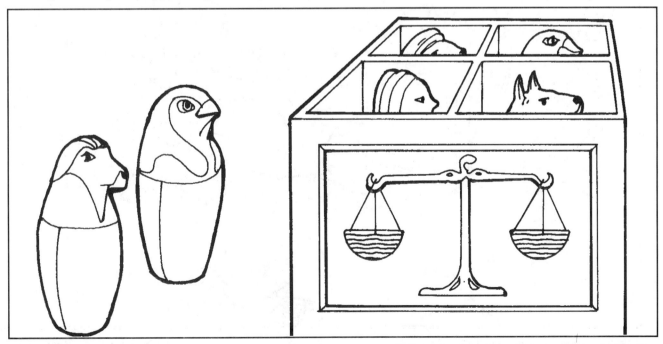

Beshet the Burial Priest *(cont.)*

Hapun: Imset will now rub the body with cedar oil, cumin, wax, natron, gum, wine, and milk. He then dusts the body with crushed spices, such as myrrh and cassia. In order for the spirits to recognize the body, we make it look lifelike by padding the cheeks and eye sockets with linen. Finally, it is time to plug the nose and close the eyelids. We then cover the body with molten resin from local trees, which turns very black as it dries and hardens.

Imset: The last stage is to paint on eyebrows and wrap the body in linen. Damutef is our expert in this final ritual.

Damutef: Wrapping the body usually requires about 150 yards of linen. The attention to details while wrapping depends on the social class of the individual. Someone from a higher class will have each finger, toe, and limb individually wrapped before wrapping the body as a whole. About 100 protective amulets or pieces of jewelry are placed inside the bandages to strengthen the parts of the body.

The heart scarab represents rebirth, the pillar represents strength, and the Eye of Horus restores health. We also include fragrant herbs such as sprigs of rosemary and flower bulbs. The wrapped mummy is then brushed again with resin, and the mummy mask depicting the individual is placed over the face. The entire mummy is then placed into a coffin painted with the person's portrait so that the spirits will know where to return. During all of these steps, prayers are chanted to ensure proper preservation.

Beshet: On the day of the burial, friends and relatives come to the embalming pavilion. The corpse is carried across the Nile on a barge to the cemetery in the western desert. The funeral procession consists of priests, relatives, and professional mourners who are paid to wail and tear at their garments and hair. These actions show grief for the departed and also help ward evil away from the coffin.

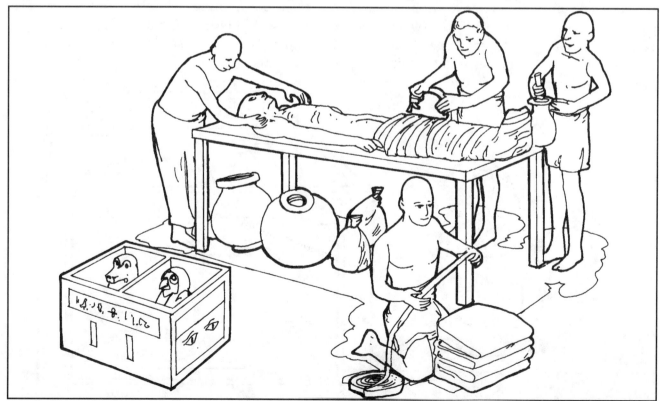

Beshet the Burial Priest *(cont.)*

Mintah: The coffin is then placed in a boat-shaped sled and drawn by oxen to the tomb. It is attended by two women mourners who represent the goddesses Isis and Nephthys. A priest waving a censer and sprinkling milk heads the procession. Behind the coffin comes the chest containing the canopic jars, followed by the person's belongings that are to be buried with the body and used in the afterlife.

Narrator 3: The Egyptians believed that in their afterlife was a paradise known as the **Field of Reeds**. In this version of heaven the grain grew tall and the fruit was plentiful. The dead were required to plow and tend to these fields to keep everything in order. Therefore, small statues called shabtis, or "little servants," were also buried in order to work for the deceased in the afterlife.

Alexus: A number of spells and incantations are said during the procession, many of them chosen by the person before death. These are taken from the ***Book of the Dead***. This book contains over 200 verses, hymns, prayers, and magic spells to help the deceased make the trip to the Underworld, pass through to the Field of Reeds, and ensure a happy afterlife. Verses from the *Book of the Dead* are also painted on the coffin, tomb walls, and papyrus scrolls.

Knunum: Once we reach the tomb, we conduct the ceremony of the **Opening of the Mouth**. We stand the coffin upright, and it is supported by a priest wearing the mask of Anubis. Priests and the eldest son of the deceased then scatter water over the coffin, burn incense, and touch the mouth of the mummy case with special magical implements. Spells are recited in which the god Ptah gives the dead person the ability to eat, speak, and move as if still alive. Offerings are made. Then the afterlife can be enjoyed, because the spirits that left the corpse during mummification can now know where to return.

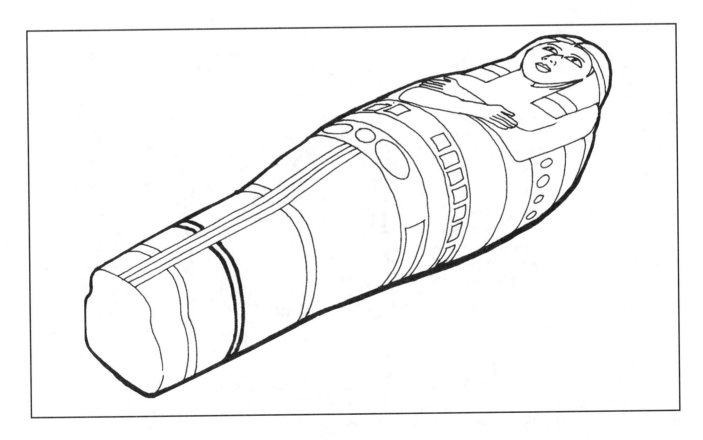

Beshet the Burial Priest *(cont.)*

Atif: The coffin is then placed in an outer coffin, which is a series of two or three other coffins painted with magical texts and illustrations to help the deceased in the Underworld. This added protection varies, depending on the person's social class. Finally, the painted coffins are placed into a large stone **sarcophagus**, and the deceased's belongings are arranged around the tomb.

Narrator 4: The upper part of the tomb consisted of a chapel where the statues and paintings were situated. Here priests and relatives could visit on anniversaries and festival days. The burial site itself was located at the bottom of a deep shaft to discourage grave robbers.

Naturik: Once the mummy and its belongings are in place, we sweep the burial chamber to remove all traces of human life and to keep it free from evil. Then we carefully seal the tomb forever. We break weapons to keep harm away from the dead. Relatives enjoy a funerary feast outside the tomb as the akh travels through the floor of the burial chamber into the Underworld and the Hall of Judgment.

Haret: Using the verses from the *Book of the Dead,* the akh moves through gateways guarded by terrifying gods such as serpents, vultures, and hippopotamuses. They stop any unworthy akh. The worthy akh reaches the Hall of Judgment, or Two Truths. Here it is judged to see if it is fit to live forever in the kingdom of Osiris and enjoy paradise in the Field of Reeds. At the **judgment scene** are Anubis, the god of mummification, who presides over the judgment; Thoth, the god of wisdom, who records the events; and a set of scales. The heart of the deceased is put on one side of the scale, where it is weighed against Ma'at or her feather of truth.

Imset: Forty-two gods then question the heart, accusing its owner of unthinkable crimes. The heart denies all charges, but only the goddess of truth, Ma'at, can determine whether or not it is lying.

Narrator 5: Naturally, all Egyptians hope to pass this test. They always showed hearts balanced with Ma'at's truth and not weighed down with evil. This may have been a source of such phrases as having a "heavy heart" when we are troubled or feeling "lighthearted" when we are happy. The Egyptians also gave us the heart as a symbol of emotion. Imagine what Valentine's Day would be like if they had known the brain was actually our center of emotion and intelligence!

Imset: If the heart does not pass the test, it is tossed to Ammit, the Devourer of the Dead, who sits beside the scales. She gobbles it up and brings complete destruction on all parts of the soul and prevents it from going on to an afterlife. If the heart is innocent, the akh passes into the throne room of Osiris. Once blessed by Osiris, the deceased can then proceed to paradise in the Field of Reeds.

Beshet: This is a celebration of the life that will continue eternally in a perfect world, free from hardships. Death is only the gateway into this world, and by providing the dead with all of these things, we ensure that life's pleasures will continue forever.

Egyptian Gods

Name _____ Date_____

The Ancient Egyptians practiced polytheism, the worship of many gods. Their first gods represented the natural elements that affected their daily lives, such as the sun, storms, river, and death. The Egyptian people believed that each had to be encouraged and thanked in order for the people to prosper. Animals were also worshiped to help protect people.

Over time, the Egyptians thought of the gods as possessing human qualities, and therefore, they were depicted with human shapes. However, some of the gods continued to have the heads of animals. Each region in Egypt had its own special god, although gradually a few of these became worshipped throughout the land as universal gods.

The study of ancient religion is very difficult because over time, the stories and myths that were told about the gods were mixed together and changed. Therefore, many of the gods' names, duties, and characteristics can vary from place to place.

Read these selections about Ancient Egypt:

- Saba the Farmer
- Farming the Land
- Egyptian Math and Medicine
- Building the Pyramids
- Beshet the Burial Priest

In a small group brainstorm about the gods the Egyptian people turned to in time of need. Create a semantic map listing all of the gods and then describe their powers. Identify how the people believed the gods helped them.

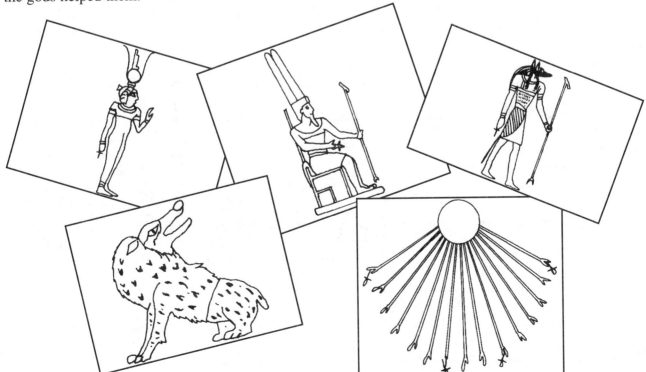

Polytheistic Stories and Myths

Name _____ Date_____

Write a story or a myth about creation and existence based on the information you have learned about the rituals and beliefs held by the Ancient Egyptians. You may include some of the gods already studied or make up new gods with new names, powers, and characteristics. Be sure to include illustrations.

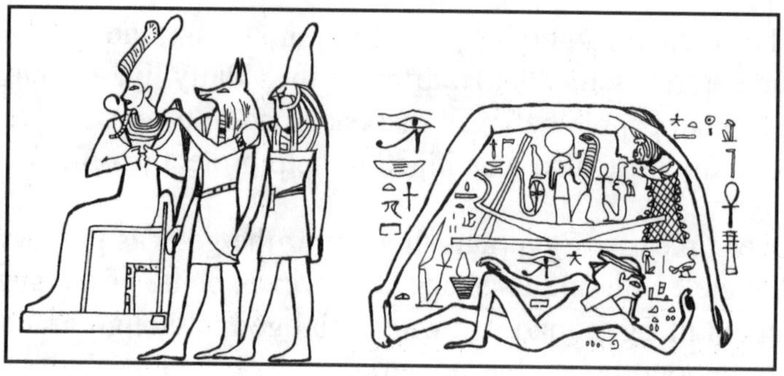

_____

_____

_____

_____

_____

_____

_____

_____

_____

_____

_____

_____

_____

_____

_____

_____

_____

The Many Egyptian Gods

Horus—son of Isis and Osiris. In mythology, he avenged the death of his father by killing Seth. During the battle he lost an eye, which was renewed by Isis. You see the Eye of Horus in paintings, amulets, and jewelry, representing renewal and protection. When people die, he leads them into the Underworld to be judged by weighing their hearts. He is sometimes depicted as the head of a falcon or as an entire falcon wearing a crown.

Osiris—one of the chief gods representing immortality. He presides over the Underworld, where he is the judge of the dead. A son of Nut and Geb, he married his sister, Isis, with whom he had a son, Horus. He is represented as a mummy in a royal crown, holding the crook and flail, the signs of sovereignty and power. Sometimes he is white (mummy wrappings), sometimes he is black (the Underworld), and sometimes he is green (spring and resurrection).

Anubis—messenger to Osiris and guard of the scales during the weighing of the heart ceremony. He is the god of embalming and presides over the mummification process. Priests wear his jackal head during rituals performed when working on a mummy.

Thoth (Troth)—the god of wisdom and science. He is the scribe of the god world, recording all writing, counting, and measurement. Since he records time, he is also the god of the moon. He is husband to Ma'at and represented by the head of an ibis. Many times he is holding tools for writing or measuring.

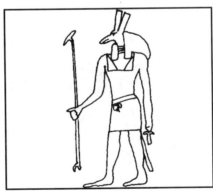

Seth (Set)—evil brother of Osiris and therefore another son of Nut and Geb. Seth represents the lord of the desert and the god of storms, violence, and disorder. His battle with Horus illustrates the battle of night with day and the conquest of good over evil. He is represented with the head of an unidentified animal.

Isis—sister and wife to Osiris, the goddess of magic and healing. She wears a headdress shaped like a seat. Some believe it is her tears for her dead husband that flood the Nile each year.

Ammit—not a god per se but a little monster who devours the souls of anyone judged impure or evil. He is part crocodile, part hippopotamus, and part lion.

The Many Egyptian Gods *(cont.)*

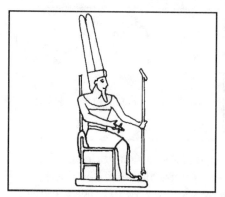

Re/Amon/Amon-Re (Ra, pronounced ray)—the original god of the sun. He sails his boat across the sky between heaven and earth. Amon is the chief god in Thebes, the capital of Egypt during the New Kingdom. Eventually Re and Amon merged together to make Amon-Re, the supreme state god of Egypt. He is usually depicted with a large crown. Sometimes the crown also has the sun disc. Many pharaohs during the New Kingdom are also shown wearing this crown, representing their devotion to Amon-Re.

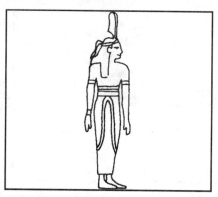

Ma'at—goddess of law and order and truth and balance. The Egyptians required precise order in their daily lives; they believed that without this balance and harmony, the world would be filled with destruction and chaos. Ma'at is the daughter of Re and wife of Thoth. The ostrich feather she wears on her head is put on the scales during the judgment ceremony. Sometimes Ma'at is shown sitting on the tip of the scales, and sometimes her entire body is being weighed on the scales itself.

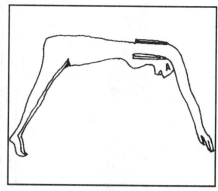

Nut—represents the heavens as the sky goddess. She is sister and wife to Geb and mother of Osiris and Seth. Nut is believed to be one of the first gods. Usually she is represented as a lady arching over the earth god, Geb. Sometimes she is seen as a large cow, and sometimes she is depicted with stars, representing the night sky.

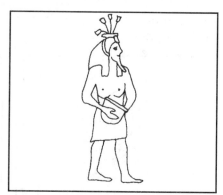

H'apy (Hapi)—god of the Nile and responsible for the proper workings of this precious river. He is usually shown as a long-haired man with papyrus and lotus flowers growing from the top of his head. He also has the chest of a woman, depicting fertility. He lives in a cave at the head of the Nile.

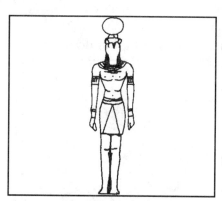

Re-Harakhti—merging of Horus and Re. Just as Amon-Re became the supreme state god, Re-Harakhti became seen as one of the sun gods. The falcon had the sun disc on his head, showing that he flies across the sky, carrying the sun.

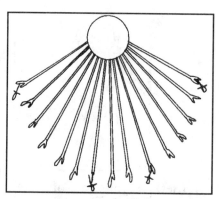

Aten—another form of the sun god, this god is unlike any of the others—neither human nor animal. This sun disc with outstretched arms holds an ankh, representing everlasting life. He is the one and only god worshiped during the reign of King Akhenaten.

The Many Egyptian Gods *(cont.)*

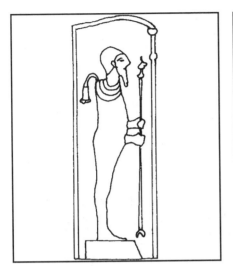

Ptah—local god of Memphis, one of the ancient capitals of Egypt, and husband to Sekhmet. He is the parson of craftsmen, since it is believed that he invented the arts. He is shown as a hairless mummylike figure holding a large tool, and at the opening of the mouth ceremony during mummification, he uses the tool he holds.

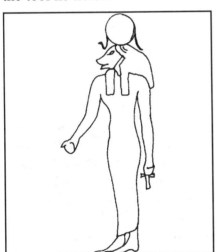

Sakhnet—brings destruction to all enemies of Re. She is the goddess of war and consulted by pharaohs. It was believed that her fiery breath was the hot winds of the Egyptian desert. She is wife to Ptah and has the head of a lion.

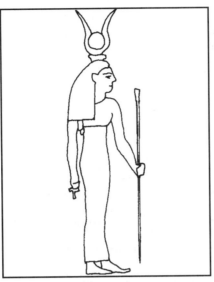

Hathor—goddess of love, beauty, dancing, and music and protector of children and birth. She is often shown as a beautiful woman with the sun disc and horns of a cow. Sometimes she is depicted as a cow with the sun disc between her horns.

Nepthys—the nature goddess who represents the day, both before sunrise and after sunset. She is daughter of Nut and Geb, sister to Isis, wife to Seth, and mother of Anubis by Osiris. She wears on her head hieroglyphics that mean "lady of the house."

Geb (Seb)—the god of the earth. He usually poses below his sister/wife, Nut. Sometimes he is shown with a goose on his head, representing one of the many creation myths in which he laid the egg from which the world sprang.

Mut—goddess of Thebes and a great divine mother. She is pictured with the head of a vulture or a vulture headdress.

Bastet (Bast)—household goddess representing joy and music. She is depicted as a cat—a prized animal in Ancient Egypt because rodents infested the granaries.

Group Mapping Activity

After reading "The Many Egyptian Gods" have students create a map that explains the relationships between the many gods and what they believe to be the important concepts and ideas from the text. Students should not talk to classmates or look back at the text.

1. Have students share their maps with a partner or members in a small group.

> Remind students to explain the following:
> - what they chose to include
> - how they chose to design their maps
> - why they made their specific choices

2. Have students work collaboratively in partners or small groups to finish their maps.

3. Encourage students to review the text to clarify questions or information.

Sample Group Map for Egyptian Gods

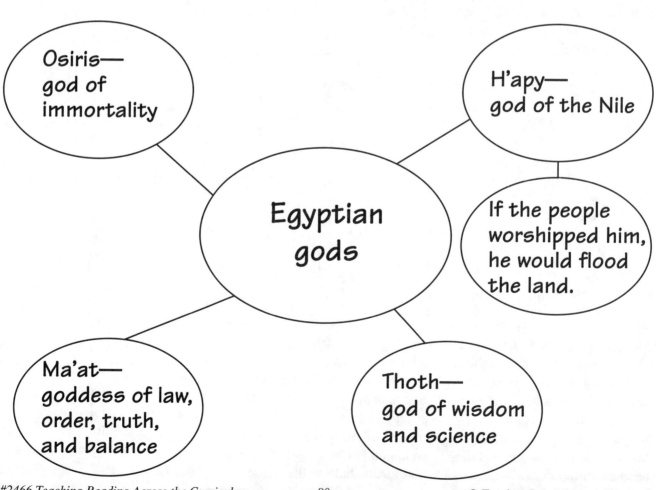

K-W-L Plus Worksheet

Name _____ Date_____

Use this K-W-L Plus worksheet during a class discussion to brainstorm what you know and what you want to know about Ancient Greece. The third column will be completed at the end of the unit, as part of a culminating activity. Here are some topics to consider as you begin your worksheet.

- Cyclops
- Mt. Olympus
- Zeus
- Macedonia
- Greco-Roman Period
- Hercules
- Trojan War

For this activity you will also break into groups and create concept maps, using the information you already know. As the unit continues you can fill in new information.

K What I Know	**W** What I Want to Know	**L** What I Learned

Ancient Greece Concept Map

Name _____ Date_____

Based on what you already know about Ancient Greece, fill in the concept map and add boxes if you want to. Work in partners to fill in additional information from the K-W-L Plus worksheet. On page 83 explain the relationships between the main concept and the other ideas and concepts you have added to the web.

Ancient Greece

Ancient Greece Conceptual Relationships

Use this page to explain the relationships among the main concept, Ancient Greece, and the other ideas, mythical gods, and events you have added to your concept web. Be sure to make the connection and the integration clear so that as you add more information, you do not become confused.

My ideas are connected to the main concept of Ancient Greece in the following ways:

_____

_____

_____

_____

_____

_____

_____

_____

_____

_____

_____

_____

_____

_____

_____

_____

_____

Map of Ancient Greece

Name _____ Date_____

In preparation for the text selections about Ancient Greece, it is important to know the geographical locations of the ancient cities and the bodies of water. Use the map of Ancient Greece on this page to locate and label the cities, islands, and bodies of water of Ancient Greece. Use other reference books such as an atlas, an encyclopedia, or information found on the Internet to locate and label the following places on the map.

Once you have located these important places, go back and add information to your concept map. You may also want to explain the importance of each location in your journal or learning log. Afterwards, compare it with a map of modern Greece and record the changes in your journal or learning log.

- Crete
- Rhodes
- Ithaca
- Sparta
- Troy
- Corinth
- Thebes
- Athens
- Mediterranean Sea
- Ionian Sea
- Aegean Sea
- Mount Olympus
- Knossos
- Delphi
- Olympia
- Pella

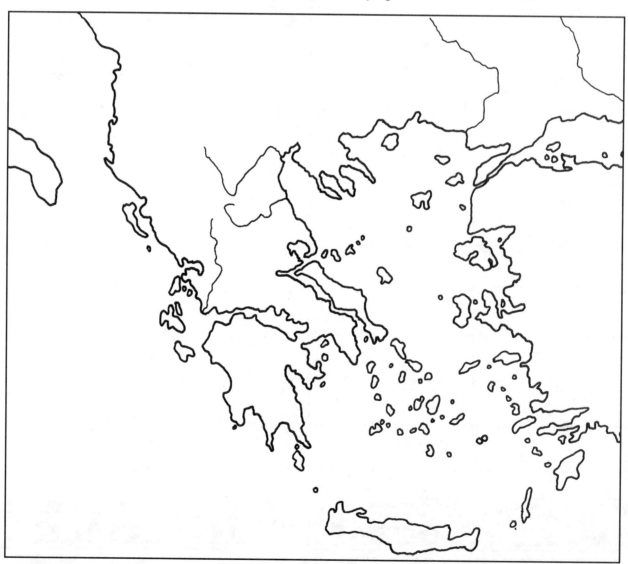

Semantic Feature Analysis

Name _____ Date_____

Use the chart below to create a semantic feature analysis about several of the ancient Greek heroes. List the heroes vertically on the left and various characteristics of heroes on the top horizontal row. Fill in the grid matching the hero with the characteristic, marking a positive sign (+) for those features that match and a negative sign (–) for the features that do not match. Add the descriptions and explanations in the appropriate boxes.

Heroes	Characteristics		

Ancient Greece Word Sleuths

Name _____ Date_____

Imagine you are a word sleuth investigating the origins and meanings of words, terms, phrases, word families, and concepts. Collect the words from the various text selections about Ancient Greece, the first Olympic games, and ancient Greek heroes, as well as your own research. Record your words and investigative findings in your vocabulary log or your learning log. Remember to look for borrowed words from other languages and cultures.

Word	Origin	Meaning

The Olympic Games

Name _____ Date_____

Use this K-W-L Plus worksheet during a class discussion to brainstorm what you know and what you want to know about the Olympic Games. The third column will be completed at the end of the unit, as part of a culminating activity. Here are some topics to consider as you begin your worksheet.

- Olympic Traditions
- Athletes
- Events
- Olympic Oath
- Olympic Torch
- Host Cities

For this activity you will also break into groups and create concept maps using the information you already know. As the unit continues you can fill in new information.

K What I Know	W What I Want to Know	L What I Learned

The Olympic Games Concept Map

Name _____ Date_____

Based on what you already know about the Olympic Games, fill in the concept map and add boxes if you want to. Some ideas are provided to get you started. Work with partners to fill in additional boxes of information from the K-W-L Plus worksheet. On page 89 explain the relationships between the main concept and the other ideas and concepts you have added to the web.

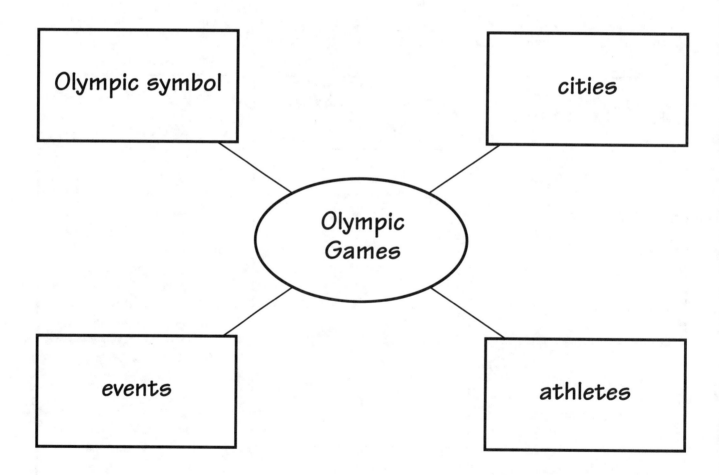

Olympic Games Conceptual Relationships

Name _____ Date_____

Use this page to explain the relationships among the main concept, the Olympic Games, and the other ideas, rituals, athletes, and events you have added to your concept web. Be sure to make the connection and the integration clear so that as you add more information you do not become confused.

My ideas are connected to the main concept of the Olympic Games in the following ways:

_____

_____

_____

_____

_____

_____

_____

_____

_____

_____

_____

_____

_____

_____

_____

_____

_____

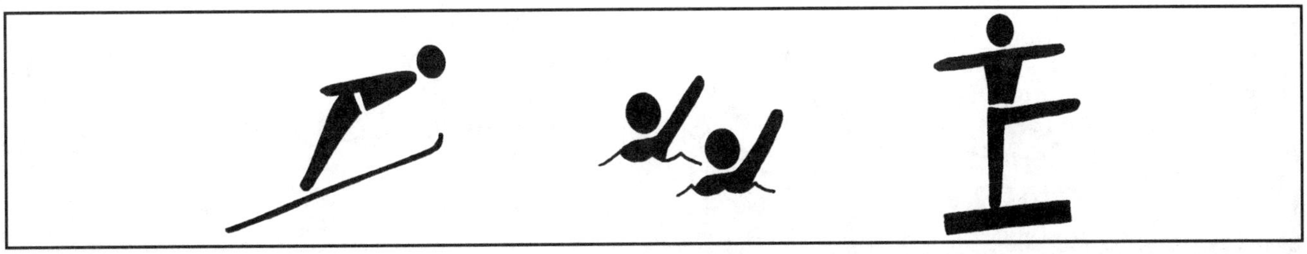

_____

_____

_____

_____

The Olympic Games: Question-Answer Relationships

For many years the ancient Greeks gathered in the beautiful Valley of Olympia to offer sacrifices to their gods. In time, this practice came to include games and contests. These games and contests came to be known as the Olympic Games, with their first recorded date being 776 B.C. The Games were held every four years until 394 A.D. This means the ancient Olympic Games lasted more than 1,000 years.

These Games, the world's oldest sports festival, became a highlight of Grecian life. All Greek male citizens were invited to participate. In time of war temporary truces were granted. Athletes and spectators from warring Greek cities were assured safe passage to the Valley of Olympia.

Athletes and judges went to Olympia for months of training before the Games opened. They trained hard and ate well. Over six pounds of meat was not an unusual dinner for an Olympian after a day's training.

The first 13 Olympics featured only one event—a foot race run one *stade*, the length of the stadium. This was approximately 200 meters (656 feet), the distance used to determine the basic length of future Olympic races, even in modern times.

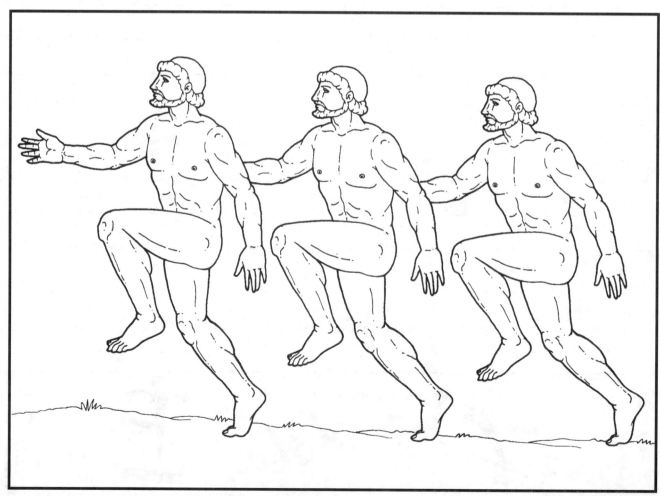

The Olympic Games: Question-Answer Relationships *(cont.)*

As time passed, additional events were added. Eventually the Olympic Games became a five-day festival. From the schedule, it is evident that the Games were deeply rooted in the religion of the people.

Day one was a day of preparation. Sacrifices were made to Zeus, the king of the Greek gods. The athletes took the Olympic oath, swearing to compete fairly. Judges also promised to be fair and just. Competitors were assigned to the events, and a contest was held for trumpeters.

Day two opened with more sacrifices to the gods. Then came the chariot race. The low, two-wheeled chariots were drawn by four horses. Two horses were harnessed to the chariot. The other two were tethered to these horses and, as the race started, ran out in front. This race of sometimes 50 chariots was the most dangerous Olympic event ever held. The racers had no lanes or barriers. There were often locked wheels, overturned chariots, even head-on collisions. A somewhat calmer bareback horse race completed the morning's program. The afternoon featured the pentathlon. Some historians believe this was an elimination contest. Those qualifying in the long jump event went on to throw a javelin, and the four best at this ran the one-stade race. The three top runners were left for the discus throw, and the final two wrestled to the finish. Others who have studied the ancient Olympics believe the winner was decided after the first three events, the others having already been eliminated.

Day three opened with more religious ceremonies. Food was eaten at a great banquet. In the afternoon boys competed in races, boxing, and upright wrestling where the object was to throw the opponent to the ground.

Day four featured the men's running events. They ran one-stade, two-stade, and 24-stade races, races similar to those run by boys. In the afternoon there was boxing, wrestling, and the pankration, a savage and sometimes deadly sport that combined wrestling, boxing, and judo. The rules forbade only biting and gouging the opponent's eyes. Breaking an opponent's finger was also condemned. Athletes often forgot their oaths of good sportsmanship in their eagerness to defeat an opponent. Yet, watchful judges had their rods ready to land vigorous taps on the athletes' heads to remind them of the rules. The final event was the *hoplite*. Here runners suited up in coats of armor to run a distance of two stades.

Day five included more sacrifices to the gods. Winners crowned with olive leaves were presented to the people. A herald would call out each person's name, the name of his proud father, and the place from which he came.

Women and girls were excluded from participating in the Olympic Games and were not allowed to watch, one reason being that the men competed nude. In time, separate races were set up for women and girls in a neighboring city. These games were known as the Herannic Games in honor of Hera, the wife of Zeus. They were held regularly, two years after each Olympic Games.

When the Roman Empire conquered Greece, the Olympic Games became less important. They ended in 394 A.D. by order of Emperor Theodosius. In time, earthquakes, floods, and landslides buried the site of the ancient festival.

The Olympic Games: Question-Answer Relationships *(cont.)*

Use the following QAR chart to reinforce this strategy with the students.

In the Book

Right There

In what year were the first Olympic Games held?

Think and Search

How long were the games held before Emperor Theodosious decided to end them?

In My Head

Author and You

What was the religious purpose of the games?

On My Own

How do the modern Olympic Games reflect the traditions set forth in the first Olympic Games?

Have students read the next selection and complete the QAR on page 95. Have students add the page to their learning logs. Ask students to share their answers and decisions in a whole-class discussion.

The Olympic Games: Question-Answer Relationships *(cont.)*

The site of the ancient Olympic Games lay buried until an archaeologist named Richard Chandler unearthed it in 1766. However, he was unable to pay for further excavation. In 1820 French archaeologists continued the work, uncovering the temple of Zeus. In 1875 German archaeologists started a six-year project that unearthed the entire city of Olympia. A French nobleman, Garon Pierre de Coubertin, became interested in their findings and visited the site. Coubertin loved sporting events and was fascinated by the ideals of the ancient Games. He believed that an international sports competition could promote world peace, and his efforts led to the formation of the International Olympic Committee.

The first modern Games were held in 1896 in Athens, Greece. Since then, with only three exceptions, they have been held every four years in different cities around the world. The exceptions have been 1916, 1940, and 1944. No Olympics took place in those years because of World Wars I and II.

Every effort has been made to vary the sites every four years. The 1904 Olympiad was held in St. Louis, Missouri. As boats and trains were the only means of transportation, the travel time for the majority of athletes and spectators attending was many, many days. The same held true for the 1932 Games held in Los Angeles, California. In the first half of the twentieth century, transportation to and from America was slow and expensive. Therefore, most Olympiads were held in Western Europe, where they were more easily accessible for the greatest number of athletes and spectators.

In 1900, polo was introduced, bringing horses back to the Games. Gradually, other sports and events were added. The winner's medal came to be cast in gold. These early Games included recognition of competitors in areas other than sports, and prizes were awarded in fine arts from 1912 through 1948. Today many host cities include a festival of the fine arts which runs in conjunction with the Olympic Games.

Although figure skating and ice hockey had been events in previous Games, the first official Winter Games to feature these events was in 1924. Their scheduling brought about another change in 1992 when it was decided that the Winter Games would be held again in 1994 and every four years thereafter—1998, 2002, etc.

The Summer Games would continue in years divisible by 4—1996, 2000, etc. Having the Summer and Winter Games in different years is a bonus for a few athletes who train for both Games and for sports fans who will be able to watch the Olympics every other year.

Another change over the years is the faces of the competitors. In 1900 women began to compete in lawn tennis, archery was added for them in 1904, and swimming was included in 1912. Today women medal in almost all phases of competition.

The growth of technology has also touched the Games. In 1912 the judging of race results was aided by electrical timers, in 1932 a type of electronic device was introduced, and in 1936 the Olympics were broadcast by radio for the first time and televised to theaters in Berlin. Televised coverage began with the 1960 Games in Rome, when images of Olympic events were broadcast into homes around the world. Thanks to television, people who had never heard of the Olympics became overnight fans, and popularity continues to grow with each competition.

The Olympic Games: Question-Answer Relationships *(cont.)*

Male athletes were housed in their own Olympic village for the first time in the 1932 Games in Los Angeles. Featured were separate dining rooms for each nation, entertainment facilities, and a lounge where visitors could mingle with the athletes. Female athletes were housed in nearby hotels. Spectators gathered daily outside the village, and a true sense of friendship existed among various nationalities.

The Olympics have grown in numbers of both participants and spectators. The competitions now last 16 days. Over 2,500 athletes attended the last Winter Games. They competed for gold, silver, and bronze medals in more than 50 events. More than 10,000 athletes attended the Summer Games in 1992. They competed for gold, silver, and bronze medals in more than 250 events. There are 180 nations that have Olympic committees.

There have been some rocky moments in the history of the Games. For example, the Games of 1936 in Berlin, Germany, collided with politics in the form of German Nazi leader Adolph Hitler. Despite boycott threats from American Jews justifiably angered by Hitler's outrageous policies, the Games went ahead as planned. Hitler certainly had not planned on the participation of American track superstar Jesse Owens, the supposedly "inferior" African-American who raced to four gold medals—and international acclaim—in Berlin. In 1972, at the Summer Games in Munich, West Germany, a terrorist attack marred the competition. Arab terrorists held as hostages and then killed 11 athletes from the Israeli Olympic Team.

At times countries have boycotted the Games because of opposing political views. A major Olympic boycott occurred in 1980 when the United States led several nations in staying away from the Moscow Games. This was to protest the Soviet Union's invasion of Afghanistan. In 1984, the Soviets led a boycott of the Los Angeles Games in an attempt to get even.

Since then, there has been a positive change in world events. The future for full attendance at upcoming Games looks hopeful.

In spite of all the changes, the ideals of the Olympic Games are the same. They are held in the hope of promoting world peace, understanding, and fair and friendly athletic competition.

The Olympic Games: Learning Log

Name _____ Date_____

Question-Answer Relationships

Title of text selection _____

In the Book QARs

_____

_____

_____

_____

_____

In My Head QARs

_____

_____

_____

_____

_____

_____

_____

_____

_____

_____

Olympic Games Concept Webs

Name _____ Date_____

Create two concept webs about the Olympic Games based on the information found in "The Olympic Games in Ancient Greece" and "The Olympic Games in Modern Times." Use these concept webs to analyze the similarities and differences between the Olympic Games in Ancient Greece and the Olympic Games in modern times. Be sure to include all of the concepts and ideas important to this major world event. Use as many boxes as you need to complete your web. Add boxes as needed.

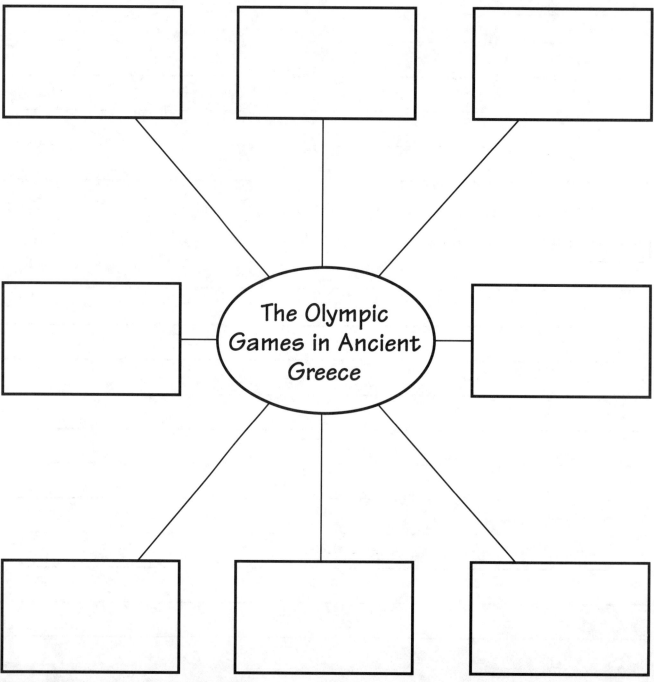

Olympic Games Concept Webs (cont.)

Name _____ Date_____

See page 96 for directions.

The Olympic Games in Modern Times

Olympic Comparisons

Name _____ Date_____

Use the semantic feature analysis below to compare the Olympic games in ancient Greece to the Olympic games in modern times. Be sure to compare the rituals, the events, and the athletes who competed in the Olympic Games.

Use the vertical column on the left to list the Olympic games held in ancient Greece and in modern times. Fill in the grid, matching the games with the characteristics (rituals, events, athletes) and marking a positive sign (+) for those features that match and a negative sign (-) for those features that do not match. Add the descriptions in the appropriate boxes.

Olympic Games	Rituals	Events	Athletes
Ancient Greece			
Modern Times			

Directed Inquiry Activity on Olympic Traditions

Name _____ Date_____

Before you read the text selections about Olympic traditions, "Opening and Closing Ceremonies," "The Olympic Symbol," and "The Olympic Torch," make predictions by answering the questions below. Record your responses on the lines provided. Add your complete responses to your learning log or your Olympian's Journal.

- What is the significance of the opening ceremonies?

  _____

  _____

- How does one declare the Games officially open?

  _____

  _____

- What is the role of the host country?

  _____

  _____

- How do the closing ceremonies differ from the opening ceremonies?

  _____

  _____

- What is the Olympic symbol and how did it orginate?

  _____

  _____

- Why is the Olympic torch so important to the Olympic Games?

  _____

  _____

After you read the selection, go back and revise your responses and predictions. Share your responses with your partner or in small groups.

Create a semantic map representing the complex relationships among the main ideas, concepts, and historical information from this text selection.

Directed Inquiry Activity on
Olympic Traditions *(cont.)*

Describe the art and music of the Olympic games.

_____

_____

_____

How was the Olympic symbol created?

_____

_____

_____

If I were an Olympic athlete…

_____

_____

_____

How do the ancient and modern games differ?

_____

_____

_____

Explain the significance of the Olympic traditions, including the opening and closing ceremonies, the torch, the symbol, and the oath.

_____

_____

_____

_____

Describe your sport, how you trained, and your performance in the Olympics.

_____

_____

_____

The changes in the ancient and modern games include…

_____

_____

_____

_____

Opening and Closing Ceremonies

Opening Ceremonies

In ancient Greece the first day of Olympic competition opened with judges in royal purple robes, a heralder, and a trumpeter entering the Hippodrome, the oval track used for the races. The judges took their stand, and the competitors in chariots drawn by four prancing horses paraded past them. The herald called out each competitor's name, the name of his father, and his city. Then the herald declared the Games officially open.

More than 2,500 years later, on a cool afternoon in 1896, another opening ceremony took place. Parading into the stadium in Athens, Greece, were 258 athletes from 13 different countries. Along with the 70,000 spectators in the stands, they heard the King of Greece declare the Games of the first modern Olympiad officially open.

The opening ceremonies have continued as a grand highlight of the Games. With television carrying its imagery around the world, the pageantry has grown. Each host city stages a spectacular performance of music, dance, and special effects. Local citizens, young and old, perform together to welcome the world to their city.

Athletes from each participating country parade into the stadium, following their national flag. Each flag is carried by the athlete chosen by his or her teammates to lead the delegation. As each team passes the reviewing stand, the flagbearer dips the flag in honor of the head of state of the host country.

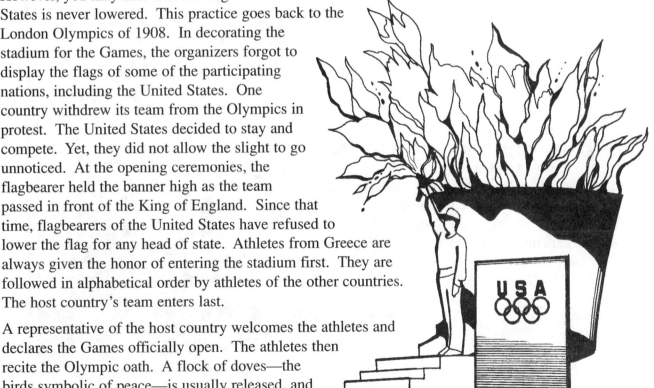

However, you may note that the flag of the United States is never lowered. This practice goes back to the London Olympics of 1908. In decorating the stadium for the Games, the organizers forgot to display the flags of some of the participating nations, including the United States. One country withdrew its team from the Olympics in protest. The United States decided to stay and compete. Yet, they did not allow the slight to go unnoticed. At the opening ceremonies, the flagbearer held the banner high as the team passed in front of the King of England. Since that time, flagbearers of the United States have refused to lower the flag for any head of state. Athletes from Greece are always given the honor of entering the stadium first. They are followed in alphabetical order by athletes of the other countries. The host country's team enters last.

A representative of the host country welcomes the athletes and declares the Games officially open. The athletes then recite the Olympic oath. A flock of doves—the birds symbolic of peace—is usually released, and the Olympic flame is lit. The ceremonies usually conclude with an explosion of breathtaking fireworks.

Opening and Closing Ceremonies (cont.)

Closing Ceremonies

After sixteen days of intense athletic competition, the setting of new world records, and the winning or losing of medals by the world's best athletes, the Olympic playing fields fall silent. As in the beginning, these Olympic athletes gather together for a ceremonial goodbye. This spectacular event is the closing ceremony of the Olympics. The athletes enter the stadium one last time to say goodbye to their fans, congratulate the winners, and celebrate the Olympic experience. The athletes are seen entering the stadium walking side by side, celebrating their new friendships, many times with competitors from other countries.

As the athletes gather together, representatives from the host country share parting thoughts of the games. The flag from the country hosting the next Olympics is raised, and representatives from that country are welcomed to the podium, to invite the world to their country in four years for the next Olympics. Finally, the Olympic Games are declared officially closed, the Olympic flame is extinguished, and the Olympic flag is lowered. Following this emotional ceremony, there is a variety of entertainment, and once again the night sky explodes with fireworks.

Activity:

Host cities begin to plan their spectacular opening and closing ceremonies years in advance. Watch videos of past festivities, then divide your class into groups to plan new ceremonies. Let them present their plans— complete with visuals and music—to an "Olympic Planning Committee" for review.

The Olympic Symbol

The five rings, the familiar symbol of the Olympic Games, were discovered by archaeologists. They found them engraved on an altar uncovered during the excavation at Delphi, Greece. It has been suggested that they were used as a symbol of the Olympics, the rings on either end indicating the year of the Games and the three rings in the middle representing the years in between. This seems a bit confusing, but the Greeks used both the solar and lunar calendars and were aware of some extra time between years. It was possibly similar to our leap year.

Baron de Coubertin, who helped initiate the modern Olympics, used the rings to symbolize the five continents of the world. These probably included North and South America (counted as one), Europe, Asia, Africa, and Australia. He chose the colors blue, yellow, black, green, and red because the flag of each competing nation has at least one of these colors.

The colored rings placed on a background of white became the design for the Olympic flag. Although displayed in Paris, France, a few years before, it was first flown at the Olympic Games in Antwerp, Belgium, in 1920. Since then it has been raised at the opening ceremonies of each successive Olympics.

Working in a group with four of your classmates, use the ring pattern below to construct a large Olympic flag.

The Olympic Torch

The lighting of the Olympic flame marks the climax of each opening ceremony. This practice can be traced back to the Olympics of the ancient Greeks. There, the priests placed sacrifices on an altar and prepared to set them on fire. Some 200 meters away, a group of young Grecian boys waited for the signal to start their foot race. The winning runner seized the flaming torch from the priest's hand and lit the sacrificial fire.

The tradition of lighting an Olympic torch in Olympia, Greece, has been a part of the modern Games for many years. Several weeks before the opening of each Olympics, the flaming torch begins its journey over land and sea to the site of the competition. Once it reaches the host country, a series of runners carry it in relays to the Olympic site. It is a very special honor to be one of these runners.

At the opening ceremonies of the Games, the torch is carried into the stadium. It is then passed to the final runner, a specially chosen citizen of the host country, often a former Olympian. He or she then climbs the stairs to the top of the stadium and tilts the torch to light the large flame that will burn throughout the Games.

Since the first torch was carried by relay runners to the Berlin Games of 1936, Olympic torches have made lengthy and interesting journeys to the Game sites. Here are the stories of a few of their trips.

In 1948 the torch made the journey of 300 km (186 miles) from Olympia to London, England, in 12 days. It was carried mostly by runners and crossed the English Channel on a warship of the Royal Navy.

In 1956, 3,500 torchbearers participated in a run from Olympia to Athens, Greece. There, the flame was put into a miner's lamp and flown to Cairns, Australia. From there it went on to Sydney and finally to the Game site of Melbourne. Australia is a big continent, and the distance covered on that land alone was 4,556 km (2,825 miles). It took 2,830 runners 13 days and nights to complete the journey.

In 1968 the torch was carried first from Greece to Spain. There it was put aboard a ship that followed the route of Columbus to the New World. It finally reached its destination of Mexico City in time for the Summer Games.

The most spectacular torch run probably took place in 1960. Walt Disney was called upon to stage the opening ceremonies at Squaw Valley, California. His plan included flying the Olympic torch from Olympia to Los Angeles by jet. There it was taken to the Los Angeles Coliseum, site of the 1932 Opening Ceremonies. It was met by 600 high school athletes who each ran a mile through California cities to the foot of the hills of Squaw Valley. Then a helicopter lifted the torch to the top of the ski slope where a skier waited to race it down the mountain. He passed it to a champion speed skater who carried it for a final lap around the stadium oval before lighting the flame. Despite a blinding snowstorm on opening day, all went according to plan. The flame burned brightly for the 16 days of those Winter Olympics.

The Olympic Torch *(cont.)*

Now it is your turn to carry the torch. Use the world map on page 106 to trace the route of the torch from Olympia, Greece, to each of the sites on page 104. Use a different color to mark each route.

Choose another color to trace the route of the torch from Olympia to the site of the most recent Olympic Games. Use the map scale to approximate how far it traveled.

Suppose you were chosen to be the final runner to carry the torch to light the Olympic flame. Write a newspaper article about your big day.

Fill the outline of the torch below with words you believe represent the spirit of the Olympics.

World Map

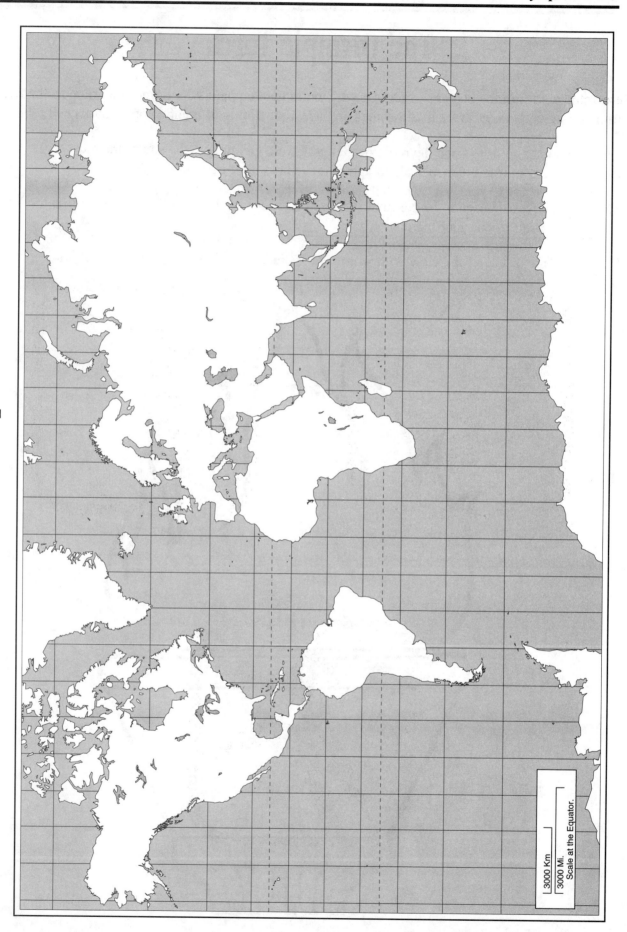

3000 Km
3000 Mi.
Scale at the Equator.

Olympic Art

Research the art associated with the Olympics, such as the Olympic symbol, the logos for each sport, mascots from various Olympic games, country flags, and the Olympic medals.

- Choose a sport to research and explore the origin of the sport, how it is played, and are some of the famous Olympians are who participated in that sport.

- Create your own illustrations for symbols and mascots for the future 2000 Olympics in Sydney, Australia.

LUGE

BIATHLON

FIGURE SKATING

Olympic Art *(cont.)*

ICE HOCKEY

BOBSLED

SKIING

SPEEDSKATING

ATHLETICS

ARCHERY

Olympic Art *(cont.)*

BASKETBALL

BASEBALL

BOXING

CANOE/KAYAK

CYCLING

DIVING

Olympic Art *(cont.)*

EQUESTRIAN

FENCING

GYMNASTICS

JUDO

MEN'S FIELD HOCKEY

MODERN PENTATHLON

Olympic Art *(cont.)*

ROLLER SKATING

ROWING

SHOOTING

SOCCER

SOFTBALL

SWIMMING

Olympic Art *(cont.)*

SYNCHRONIZED SWIMMING

TABLE TENNIS

TAEKWANDO

HANDBALL

TENNIS

VOLLEYBALL

Olympic Art *(cont.)*

WATER POLO

WEIGHT LIFTING

YACHTING

WOMEN'S FIELD HOCKEY

WRESTLING

Famous Olympians

If the names of famous Olympians were placed end to end, they could probably circle the globe many times. Here is an introduction to a few who earned the gold. Perhaps you will want to find out more about them. It is hoped you will continue your search to become acquainted with still other equally famous Olympic stars.

U.S. Olympic Stars

In track and field events, the name of Jesse Owens, the sharecropper's son from Alabama, always tops the list of favorite Olympians. His four gold medals won at the 1936 Berlin Olympics discredited Hitler's notion of German superiority over other races.

In 1984 another track sensation by the name of Carl Lewis matched Jesse Owens' performance of 28 years before and went on to excel in the 1988 and 1992 Games also.

Babe Didrikson was the track star of the 1932 Olympics, capturing a gold medal for the U.S. in the javelin throw and another in the 800-meter hurdles. She went on to become a golf star and is still considered one of the most versatile athletes.

The decathlon winner usually holds the honor of being considered the world's best athlete. In 1952 Bob Mathias became the youngest man to earn the gold. Four years later he won again at the age of 21. Other honored decathlon winners include Rafer Johnson (1960), Bill Toomey (1968), and Bruce Jenner (1976).

Swimming and diving has seen its champions, too. After winning five gold medals in swimming in 1924 and 1928, Johnny Weissmuller went on to play the original Tarzan. Patricia McCormick practiced over 100 dives a day to achieve her goal. She swept the diving events for the United States in both the 1956 and 1960 Olympics. Her daughter also went on to medal in diving in the 1984 and 1988 Olympics.

Greg Louganis, protégé of the 1948 Olympic diving star Dr. Sammy Lee, won diving events in both the 1984 and 1988 Games. After winning two bronze medals in 1968, Mark Spitz came back to earn seven gold medals in swimming events in the 1972 Games.

Eddie Eagan won a gold in four-man bobsledding in 1920 and another in boxing in 1932. He is the only athlete to have won a gold medal in both winter and summer Games.

In 1980 speed skater Eric Heiden became the first to win five individual gold medals in his sport.

The sport of figure skating has brought the gold to the United States quite often. Winners include Tenley Albright (1956), Carol Heiss (1960), Peggy Fleming (1972), Dorothy Hamill (1976), and Kristy Yamaguchi (1992). Dick Button was a two-time gold medal winner for the men (1948, 1952) and continued to attend many Olympic Games as a television commentator on his sport. Alan Hayes Jenkins won a skating gold in 1956, and his brother David took it in 1960. Other men's winners include Scott Hamilton (1984) and Brian Boitano (1992).

Famous Olympians *(cont.)*

Some of the most familiar names of former Olympians are found in the boxing world. Floyd Patterson won the gold for the United States in the 1952 Games and later became the heavyweight champion of the world. George Foreman won the gold in the super heavyweight division in 1968. As a professional, he defeated the 1964 winner, Joe Frazier. Later he lost to the gold medal winner of the 1960 Games, Cassius Clay, known to boxing fans as Muhammad Ali.

Other famous Olympians include the following:

Andrea Mead Lawrence of Vermont was the first U.S. woman to win two medals in Alpine skiing.

Harrison "Bones" Dillard was considered one of the greatest hurdlers of all times. He won four gold medals for the U.S. in 1948 and 1952.

Al Oerter threw the discus to win the gold in four Olympics (1956–1968).

Patty O'Brien threw the shot put in four Olympics (1952–1964) for two gold medals and a silver medal.

Famous Olympians *(cont.)*

Foreign Stars

Leonidas of Rhodes, perhaps the greatest runner of all time, won the 200 meter, 400 meter, and hoplite in four Olympics from 164 B.C. to 152 B.C.

Paavo Nurmi, known as the "flying Finn," first competed in 1920. He won seven gold and three silver medals for Finland over three Olympics. He was known for his explosive starts and habit of boasting ahead of time about his winning performances.

Daley Thompson of Great Britain became the pride of his country by winning the decathlon in 1980 and 1984.

Dawn Fraser, Australia's popular freestyle swimmer, competed in three successive Olympics (1956, 1960, and 1964). She earned one silver and five gold medals.

Sonja Henie of Norway was only ten years old when she appeared in her first Olympics. She did not win that year, but she later won three gold medals in figure skating (1928, 1932, and 1936). After figure skating she became a popular movie star.

In 1956 Anton (Tony) Sailer became the hero of Austria as the first skier to sweep gold medals in all three Alpine events.

In 1968 Jean Claude Killy of France succeeded in repeating Sailer's feat. In 1992, he was once again in the spotlight as he secured and organized the Games for Albertville, France. These Games took place in the Alpine mountains only a few miles (km) from where Killy had grown up and first learned to ski.

The West Germans were hoping for the same three Alpine medals in 1988 from their skiing sensation, Rosi Mettermaier. She won the first two races but lost the giant slalom by only .12 of a second.

The beginning of the gymnastics craze is often credited to Olga Korbut of the Soviet Union, but she did not win a gold medal in individual event competition. Her aggressive and daring style amazed the fans at the 1972 Games. Four years later, Nadia Comaneci of Romania collected seven perfect tens (the highest score in gymnastics) and seven gold medals to reach a new level of achievement for the sport.

The continent of Africa has been the home of many brilliant runners. Abebe Bikila, used to running barefoot in his native Ethiopia, saw no reason to put on shoes as he ran the marathon in the 1960 Games. After winning the gold medal in two hours and 15 minutes, he still had enough energy to take a victory lap around the stadium. In 1964 he again won the marathon, this time wearing shoes. He is the only man in Olympic history to win two consecutive marathons.

Kipchoge Keino of Kenya won two gold and two silver medals over two Olympics (1968 and 1972). He wore a cap when he raced and delighted in tossing it to the crowd as he completed his final lap.

Famous Olympians *(cont.)*

How well do you remember the Olympic stars? Match each star below with his or her description in the opposite column. Use a ruler to draw a straight line from one to the other.

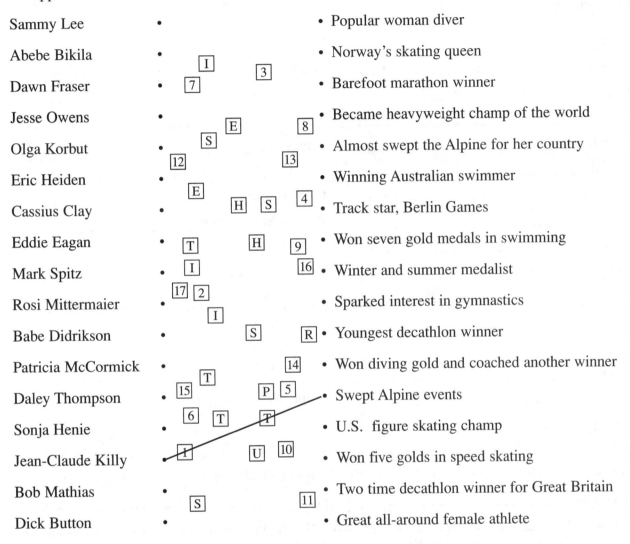

Sammy Lee	• Popular woman diver
Abebe Bikila	• Norway's skating queen
Dawn Fraser	• Barefoot marathon winner
Jesse Owens	• Became heavyweight champ of the world
Olga Korbut	• Almost swept the Alpine for her country
Eric Heiden	• Winning Australian swimmer
Cassius Clay	• Track star, Berlin Games
Eddie Eagan	• Won seven gold medals in swimming
Mark Spitz	• Winter and summer medalist
Rosi Mittermaier	• Sparked interest in gymnastics
Babe Didrikson	• Youngest decathlon winner
Patricia McCormick	• Won diving gold and coached another winner
Daley Thompson	• Swept Alpine events
Sonja Henie	• U.S. figure skating champ
Jean-Claude Killy	• Won five golds in speed skating
Bob Mathias	• Two time decathlon winner for Great Britain
Dick Button	• Great all-around female athlete

As you draw each straight line, you will notice that it passes through one square with a **number** in it and through one square with a **letter**. Below you will find a row of numbered boxes. **Place the letters in the boxes with their matching numbers.** (One is already done for you.) If you have matched all the stars correctly, you will find the answer to this riddle.

What did the ancient Olympian say when he lost his olive wreath?

1	2	3	4	5	6	7	8	9	10	11	12	13	14	15	16	17	!
T																	!

Famous Olympians (*cont.*)

Below are former Olympians with whom you may be familiar. Select one of these athletes and sign your name on the line beside your choice. Read further about this athlete and use the profile sheet to report on your findings.

Jim Abbott_____	Rafer Johnson _____
John Stephen Akhwiri_____	Michael Jordan _____
Tenley Albright _____	Jackie Joyner-Kersee_____
Abebe Bikila_____	Kipchoge Keino _____
Matt Biondi_____	Nancy Kerrigan_____
Bonnie Blair _____	Jean Claude Killy _____
Fanny Blankers-Koen _____	Olga Korbut_____
Brian Boitano _____	Andrea Mead Lawrence _____
Dick Button_____	Sammy Lee _____
Cassius Clay _____	Leonidas of Rhodes _____
Nadia Comaneci _____	Carl Lewis_____
James Connally_____	Greg Louganis_____
Rick Demont_____	Bob Mathias _____
Babe Didrikson_____	Patricia McCormick _____
Eddie Eagan _____	Ralph Metcalfe _____
Janet Evans _____	Rosi Mittemaier _____
Ray Ewry _____	Shannon Miller _____
Peggy Fleming _____	Milo of Croton _____
George Foreman _____	Paavo Nurmi _____
Dawn Fraser _____	Patty O'Brien _____
Joe Frazier_____	Al Oerter_____
Florence Griffith-Joyner _____	Jesse Owens _____
Dorothy Hamill_____	Floyd Patterson _____
Eric Heiden _____	Mary Lou Retton_____
Carol Heiss _____	Daley Thompson_____
Sonja Henie_____	Jim Thorpe _____
Dan Jansen _____	Bill Toomey_____
Alan Hayes Jenkins_____	Johnny Weissmuller _____
David Jenkins _____	Katerina Witt_____
Bruce Jenner _____	Kristy Yamaguchi _____

Famous Olympians *(cont.)*

Choose one of your favorite Olympic athletes to research and profile.

Athlete's Name: _____

Country: _____

Olympic Year(s): _____

Event(s) Won: _____

Record(s) Set: _____

Interesting facts about this athlete: _____

_____

_____

_____

_____

_____

_____

_____

_____

_____

_____

Vocabulary Self-Collection Strategy

In pairs or small groups, have students nominate one or two words or terms about which they believe the class should learn or know more. The teacher also nominates one or two words also. Have students keep a vocabulary log of new words they learn throughout the Ancient Greece/Olympic Games unit. The following words can be used to initiate the vocabulary self-collection process.

amateur	Athens, Greece	competitor
luge	Berlin, Germany	logo
oath	laurel	boycott
chariot	ceremony	delegation

Group Mapping Activity

After reading "For Amateurs Only" on pages 122 and 123, have students create a map that explains what they believe to be the important concepts and ideas from the text. Students should not talk to classmates or look back at the text. Share the sample map below with students, if necessary.

1. Have students share their maps with a partner or members in a small group.

> Remind students to explain:
>
> - what they chose to include
>
> - how they chose to design their maps
>
> - why they made their specific choices

2. Have students work collaboratively with partners or in small groups to finish their maps.

3. Encourage students to review the text to clarify questions or information.

Sample Group Map
"For Amateurs Only"

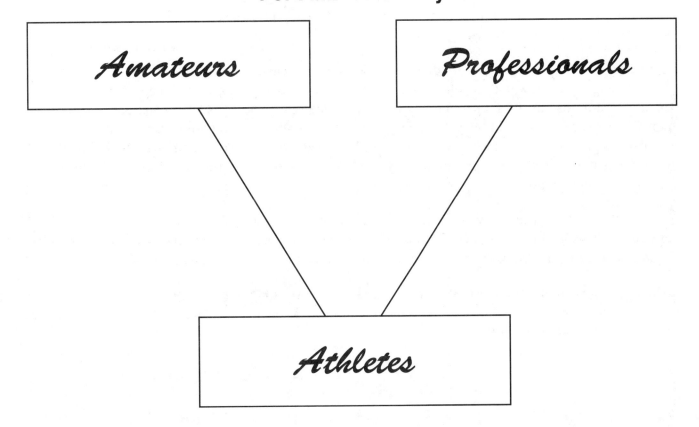

For Amateurs Only

In the 1912 Olympics, Jim Thorpe, a Native American from Oklahoma, won the pentathlon and the decathlon. To win the pentathlon he had to make the best combined score in five track and field events. The decathlon consisted of ten events. Thorpe was widely hailed in 1912 as the world's greatest all-around athlete. All this changed in 1913 when it was discovered that Thorpe had once received $15 a week to play minor league baseball, then a non-Olympic sport. His awards were sent back to the Olympic officials who offered them to the second-place winners of the pentathlon and decathlon. Both second-place winners refused to accept Thorpe's gold medals. Nevertheless, Jim Thorpe was voted by sports writers in 1950 as the greatest American athlete of the 20th century. In 1973, 20 years after the champion's death, his amateur status was reinstated by the American Athletic Union. Jim Thorpe is the most famous example of the Olympic Committee's enforcement of the rule allowing only amateur athletes as competitors.

But what was an amateur? Many found the rules confusing. Babe Didrikson, the star of the 1932 Olympics, was barred from further Olympic competition when her picture appeared in an automobile advertisement. She claimed she had received no payment, but it did not help her cause when a new red Dodge coupe showed up in her driveway. Another victim of the regulations was the great runner from Finland, Paavo Nurmi. Winner of six gold medals in 1920, 1924, and 1928, he was forbidden to compete in the 1932 Games as he had accepted money for public appearances.

In 1960 the International Olympic Committee (IOC) defined an amateur as *one who participates and always has participated solely for pleasure....and to whom participation in sport is nothing more than recreation without material gain of any kind, direct or indirect.* Clauses were added to ban athletes from many other practices, among them advertising, endorsing products, or receiving help in training from businesses or governments.

Enforcing the amateur rule against individual athletes proved easier than against entire teams or nations. The winning Japanese women's volleyball team was composed of young women kept segregated to endure vigorous, sometimes cruel, training for most of the year. For years Soviet and East European athletes were supported and trained by their governments. Even though these teams and athletes were not paid as professionals, they certainly could not be called amateur. That contributed to the joy of victory when the strictly amateur U.S. hockey teams of 1960 and 1980 were able to win gold medals against such competitors.

In 1971 the IOC dropped the word "amateur" and attempted instead to define positive rules of eligibility. This led to even more confusion. During recent years it has been left up to each individual sport's federation to make its own rules for Olympic competition.

Although defeated in 1972 and 1988, The U.S. has won more gold medals in men's basketball than has any other country. In 1992, the U.S. men's basketball team, known as the "dream team," was dominated by well-known professional players.

For Amateurs Only *(cont.)*

In 1988 tennis became an official Olympic sport, and many well-known stars took to the court in hopes of Olympic gold.

A major breakthrough for figure skaters came in 1994 when those who had turned professional were again given Olympic eligibility. This ruling saw stars such as Brian Boitano and Katerina Witt once again on Olympic ice. Some returned because they wanted to compete with the very best in the world and perhaps gain another medal. Others, realizing there were young talented athletes ready for the gold, simply wanted to renew the wonderful Olympic experience. Undoubtedly, there will continue to be changes in the future.

There are mixed feelings about allowing professional athletes and teams to compete in the Olympics. If the Games are to reflect the best talent in the world, some say, then let them come. However, there are only so many spots on each country's team. If these spots are filled with professionals, up-and-coming young athletes will miss the chance to display their talents and participate in the Olympic Games. Many of today's professional athletes might have missed their opportunity for stardom had they not first shared in Olympic glory.

Choose some members of your class who would be interested in debating the pros and cons of amateur competition. Prepare and stage a debate on the subject. Work with a group to compile a list of well-known athletes whose careers were launched by their participation in an Olympics.

Ancient Civilizations Slide Show

Studying ancient cultures is such a rewarding experience. Let your students share their findings through multimedia slide shows.

Grade Level: three to five

Duration: 60–120 minutes on the computer

Materials: pages 125–128

Procedure:

Before the Computer:

- Have your students work to research their country's focus questions (so that every focus question is answered in every slide show).

- Each of your students will create an independent slide show.

- In the classroom and media center, have your students research the following questions about their ancient civilizations:

    1. How did the ancient civilization meet its basic need for food?
    2. How did the ancient civilization meet its basic need for shelter?
    3. How did the ancient civilization meet its basic need for clothing?
    4. How did the ancient civilization meet its need for transportation?
    5. What forms of art and architecture did the ancient civilization develop?
    6. What forms of recreation did the ancient civilization develop?
    7. What advancements in science did the ancient civilization provide?

- Help your students complete their research by using the Ancient Civilizations Research Sheet.

Procedures on the Computer:

When the research is complete, use class time to plan for the slide show. There is a planning sheet available for those students who need structure and organization. You may find that some students create better slide shows when planning on their own.

Optional Activities:

- Use the above research questions to study and create projects about other civilizations.

- Expand your studies to compare the ancient times to the present.

Ancient Civilizations Slide Show *(cont.)*

ANCIENT CIVILIZATIONS RESEARCH SHEET

Civilization:_____

1. How did the ancient civilization meet its basic need for food?

   _____

   _____

   _____

2. How did the ancient civilization meet its basic need for shelter?

   _____

   _____

   _____

3. How did the ancient civilization meet its basic need for clothing?

   _____

   _____

   _____

4. How did the ancient civilization meet its need for transportation?

   _____

   _____

   _____

5. What forms of art and architecture did the ancient civilization develop?

   _____

   _____

   _____

6. What forms of recreation did the ancient civilization develop?

   _____

   _____

   _____

7. What advancements in science did the ancient civilization provide?

   _____

   _____

Other Interesting Facts:

   _____

   _____

Ancient Civilizations Slide Show *(cont.)*

Student Name: _____

Civilization: _____

ANCIENT CIVILIZATIONS PLANNING SHEET

Title Slide _____	Introduction to Slide Show _____	Food _____
Shelter _____	Clothing _____	Transportation _____

Ancient Civilizations Slide Show *(cont.)*

Student Name: _____

Civilization: _____

ANCIENT CIVILIZATIONS PLANNING SHEET *cont.*

Art and Architecture _____

Recreation _____

Advancements in Science _____

Free Choice _____

Free Choice _____

The End _____

Ancient Civilizations Slide Show *(cont.)*

Student Name:_____

ANCIENT CIVILIZATIONS PROJECT CHECKLIST

Required Contents:

The slide show was well planned.	Not Quite	Meets Goals	Way to Go!
The slide show contains a title slide.	Not Quite	Meets Goals	Way to Go!
There is an introduction to the slide show.	Not Quite	Meets Goals	Way to Go!
The slide show describes the food of the ancient civilization.	Not Quite	Meets Goals	Way to Go!
The slide show describes the shelter of the ancient civilization.	Not Quite	Meets Goals	Way to Go!
The slide show describes the clothing of the ancient civilization.	Not Quite	Meets Goals	Way to Go!
The slide show describes the transportation of the ancient civilization.	Not Quite	Meets Goals	Way to Go!
The slide show describes the art and architecture of the ancient civilization.	Not Quite	Meets Goals	Way to Go!
The slide show describes the recreation of the ancient civilization.	Not Quite	Meets Goals	Way to Go!
The slide show describes the science advancements of the ancient civilization.	Not Quite	Meets Goals	Way to Go!
The students included at least one other interesting fact.	Not Quite	Meets Goals	Way to Go!

Extras:

The student included detail and creativity in his/her artwork.	Not Quite	Meets Goals	Way to Go!
The student scanned in pictures to include in his/her presentation.	Not Quite	Meets Goals	Way to Go!
A map is included to show the location of the ancient civilization.	Not Quite	Meets Goals	Way to Go!
A bibliography is included.	Not Quite	Meets Goals	Way to Go!

Westward Expansion Unit

For this unit, the class should be divided into small groups representing different pioneer families who traveled west during the mid-1800s. Each student will assume a family role. These families will each be given a different route with the ultimate goal of reaching Sacramento, California. Throughout the unit the families will be faced with medical hardships, supply dilemmas, and many challenges particular to that time period. The objective of the unit is for students to experience and understand the difficulties of westward expansion faced by the pioneer families in the mid-1800s. The students' understanding of westward expansion will be assessed through completed activities. A westward expansion portfolio can be maintained for each student to collect samples of writing.

K-W-L Plus Worksheet

Name _____ Date_____

Use this K-W-L Plus worksheet during a class discussion to brainstorm what you know and what you want to know about the westward expansion. The third column will be completed at the end of the unit, as part of a culminating activity. Here are some topics to consider as you begin your worksheet.

- Covered Wagons
- Sacajawea
- Annie Oakley
- Cattle Trails
- Cowboys
- Native American Tribes
- Wild Bill Hickok

For this activity you will also break into groups and create concept maps, using the information they already know. As the unit continues you can fill in new information.

K What I Know	W What I Want to Know	L What I Learned

Westward Expansion Concept Map

Name _____ Date_____

Based on what you already know about westward expansion, fill in the concept map. You may add extra boxes if you want to. Work with partners to fill in additional information from the K-W-L Plus worksheet. On page 132, explain the relationships between the main concept and the other ideas and concepts you have added to the web.

Westward
Expansion

Westward Expansion Conceptual Relationships

Name _____ Date_____

Use this page to explain the relationships among the main concept, Westward Expansion, and the other ideas, people, places, and events you have added to your concept web. Be sure to make the connection and the integration clear so that as you add more information you do not become confused.

My ideas are connected to the main concept of westward expansion in the following ways:

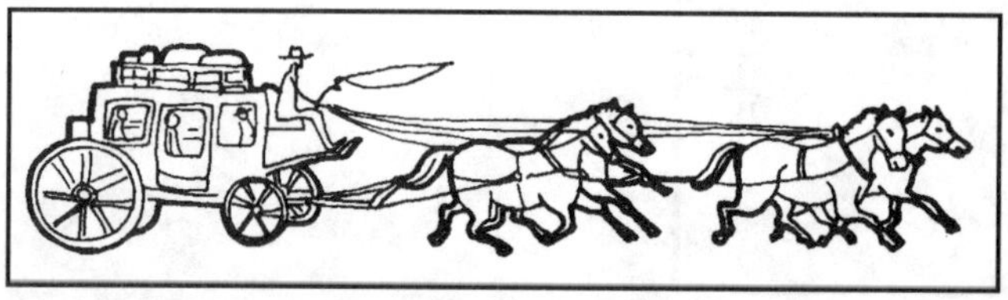

_____

_____

_____

_____

_____

_____

_____

_____

_____

_____

_____

_____

_____

_____

_____

_____

_____

Sacajawea: Question-Answer Relationships

Sacajawea, whose name means Bird Woman, was a Shoshone Indian who was born sometime around 1787. Sacajawea has been honored as one of the greatest women in American history. In 1800, Sacajawea was captured by another tribe and sold to Toussaint Charbonneau, a French-Canadian trapper. Charbonneau married Sacajawea. In 1804, two United States army officers, Meriwether Lewis and William Clark, hired Charbonneau as an interpreter and guide for an expedition to explore the Northwest. Sacajawea accompanied her husband when he joined the expedition.

Sacajawea proved to be indispensable as an interpreter and as a guide. She knew the secrets of living off the land. While crossing the Rocky Mountains, the expedition met a band of Shoshone Indians. She saved the expedition members from being harmed by the Indians. She was also able to convince the tribe to give horses and supplies for the expedition. She was an energetic member of the team and was looked after by all of the members of the group.

Sacajawea lived to be more than one hundred years old and spent her last years as an agent of good will between Native Americans and the settlers. Throughout the West, many monuments have been built to honor her. There is an especially famous statue of her in Washington Park.

Discussion Questions

1. Why do you think Sacajawea was so helpful to the members of the expedition?

2. What was exciting about this expedition? What was dangerous about it?

3. Would you want to be a guide for an expedition like this one? Explain your answer.

Sacajawea: Question-Answer Relationships *(cont.)*

Name _____ Date_____

Directions: Read the selection on page 133. Complete the following chart and add this page to your learning log. Share your answers and decisions in a whole-class discussion.

In the Book

Right There

What does the name Sacajawea mean?

_____

_____

_____

_____

_____

_____

Think and Search

To which tribe did Sacajawea belong?

_____

_____

_____

_____

_____

In My Head

Author and You

How did Sacajawea help the explorers, Lewis and Clark?

_____

_____

_____

_____

_____

_____

_____

_____

On My Own

How can Sacajawea's actions teach us about tolerance?

_____

_____

_____

_____

_____

_____

_____

Westward Expansion Daily Journal

Name _____ Date_____

During the mid-1800s many pioneers wanted to settle in the Wild West so they made their way across the mountains, prairies, and deserts to call the Wild West their new home. Gold diggers journeyed West in hopes of striking it rich. Cowboys came to the West and used the open prairie as grazing land for their cattle. Farmers came to the West and worked hard to transform the prairies into fields of crops they could sell. On their journey, they were faced with many dangers such as hostile Indians, wild animals, vicious outlaws, and treacherous weather conditions. Below is a list of daily dilemmas your pioneer family group will face on your journey west. Record your thoughts, ideas, and solutions in your daily journals.

Daily Dilemmas

On the following pages you are given a variety of daily experiences and adventures as you and your pioneer family travel west. Among the daily dilemmas you will face are the following:

- broken wagons

- crossing rivers

- illness

- encountering buffalo

- shortage of material supplies

- food shortages, reliance on nature

- unexpected deaths

- wrong directions

- sick oxen, mules, or horses

- treacherous weather conditions: snow, thunderstorms, dust storms, flooding

You will complete one dilemma activity per day. Research the lives of the pioneer families to help you respond to each daily dilemma. As you complete each page, add it to your journal notebook.

Covered Wagon Dilemma

Name _____ Date_____

Today as your family travels west it will become difficult when a wagon wheel breaks off after hitting a few ruts. Please answer the following questions in your daily journal.

- Explain, in detail, who repaired your wagon and how it was fixed. How did you contribute?

- Explain what materials were needed and how this effects your supplies list.

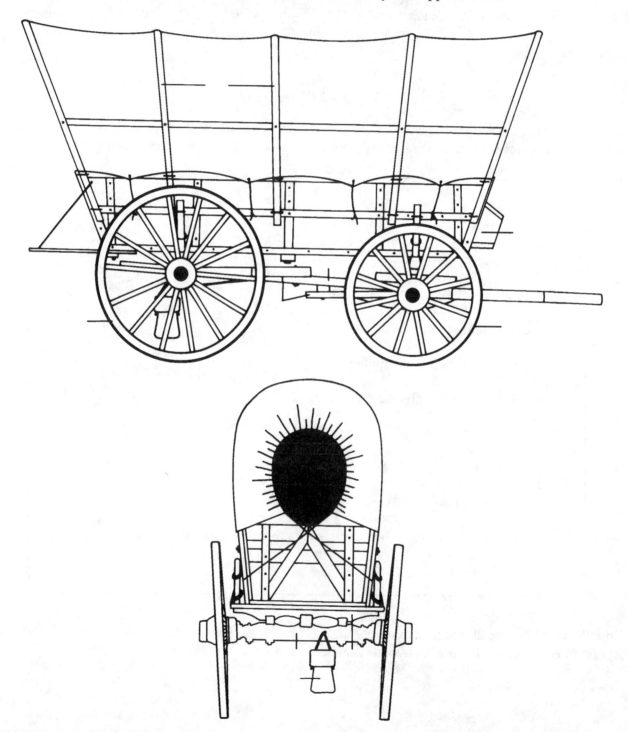

Daily Dilemma: Encountering Buffalo

Name _____ Date_____

Today as you travel, you will encounter your first few buffalos. You wonder if the herd is close by and what dangers that they bring. Discuss the following questions and record the answers below.

1. At first sighting of the buffalo, what should be done?

   _____

   _____

   _____

2. What danger does a herd present?

   _____

   _____

   _____

3. How do you kill a buffalo?

   _____

   _____

   _____

4. What benefits are derived from killing a buffalo?

   _____

   _____

   _____

Daily Dilemma: Crossing Rivers

Name _____ Date_____

Today your family has finally made it to the Humboldt River. The river looks deep in parts but passable in others. Discuss the following questions and record the answers in your journals.

1. If you feel the water is passable, what precautions will you take with the wagon?

   _____

   _____

   _____

2. If you feel the water is too deep, what are some other ways to cross the river?

   _____

   _____

   _____

3. What precautions should be taken with the animals crossing?

   _____

   _____

   _____

4. How can you work with the others on the wagon trail to cross the river?

   _____

   _____

   _____

Daily Dilemma: Unexpected Deaths

Name _____ Date_____

Today is a sad day as one of your family members is stricken with smallpox and dies. Discuss the following questions and record answers in your journals.

1. If the father of the family dies, who will take over?

_____

_____

_____

_____

2. Will you decide to continue west or return east?

_____

_____

_____

_____

3. What precautions must be taken to prevent illnesses from spreading?

_____

_____

_____

_____

Daily Dilemma: Wrong Directions

Name _____ Date_____

Today while you stopped to fix a broken wheel, your wagon train went on ahead. You are now lost. Discuss the following questions and record the answers in your journals.

1. What clues must you try to find to help you catch up to your wagon train?

_____

_____

_____

_____

_____

2. Will the Indians help you?

_____

_____

_____

_____

_____

3. You come across a shortcut. Should you use it or go the long way?

_____

_____

_____

_____

_____

Daily Dilemma: Dust Storms

Name _____ Date_____

Today, while you are crossing the plains in the hot sun, a strong west wind blows. The wind is so strong it creates some powerful dust storms. Discuss the following questions and record your answers in your journals.

1. Will the dust storms stop the wagon train? If so, then for how long?

   _____

   _____

   _____

   _____

   _____

2. How are the animals affected by these storms? What can be done to protect them?

   _____

   _____

   _____

   _____

   _____

3. How are the families affected by the dust storms?

   _____

   _____

   _____

   _____

   _____

   _____

Daily Dilemma: Weather and Flooding

Name _____ Date_____

Today, after a day of heavy rains, you find that you are experiencing some side effects caused by the weather. Discuss the following questions and record your answers in your journals.

   1. Your trail has become very muddy. Should you go on? What damage might be caused? If you decide to stop, for how long will you stop?

   _____

   _____

   _____

   _____

   _____

   _____

   _____

   2. How does the flooding affect the animals?

   _____

   _____

   _____

   _____

   _____

   _____

Daily Dilemma: Food Shortage, Reliance on Nature

Name _____ Date_____

Today you find your food supply greatly diminished. Your meat has gone bad and is full of maggots. What will you do? Discuss the following questions and record your answers in your journals.

1. What plants could you eat?

_____

_____

_____

_____

2. What wild animals could you eat?

_____

_____

_____

_____

3. Could you trade something with the Indians for meat?

_____

_____

_____

_____

Daily Dilemma: Illness

Name _____ Date_____

Today your family will be faced with its first illness. The father of the family has cholera. Discuss the following questions and record the answers in your journals.

1. How do you suspect the father has come down with cholera?

   _____

   _____

   _____

2. What precautions must be taken to avoid infecting the others members of the family?

   _____

   _____

   _____

3. How can Father be treated? Are there any doctors on the journey?

   _____

   _____

   _____

4. How much will having Father sick slow down your progress? Who will take over?

   _____

   _____

   _____

Daily Dilemma: Sick Oxen, Mules, or Horses

Name _____ Date_____

Today you find one of your oxen has a bleeding hoof. What will you do if you lose your oxen? Discuss the following questions and record your answers in your journals.

1. What first aid can you perform on your sick oxen?

   _____

   _____

   _____

   _____

   _____

2. After taking care of the infected hoof, what can you do to protect the hoof?

   _____

   _____

   _____

   _____

   _____

3. If the oxen can not continue the trip, what will happen?

   _____

   _____

   _____

   _____

   _____

Daily Dilemma: Shortage of Supplies

Name _____ Date_____

Today you realize that your supplies are running low. Your clothes and shoes are worn out. The wagon needs repairs. Discuss the following questions and record your answers in your journals.

1. What will you do to carry on your journey?

   _____

   _____

   _____

   _____

   _____

2. A fort is a few days away. What can be done at the fort?

   _____

   _____

   _____

   _____

3. Friendly Indians offer help. What can you trade with them?

   _____

   _____

   _____

   _____

   _____

Daily Dilemma: Snowstorm

Name _____ Date_____

Today, the weather takes a turn for the worse with cold temperatures and snow flurries.
Discuss the following questions and record the answers in your journals.

1. With temperatures dropping, what precautions must be taken with the wagon,
   family, clothes, food, and animals?

   _____

   _____

   _____

   _____

   _____

2. How much will the snow hinder your journey?

   _____

   _____

   _____

   _____

   _____

3. Is there a way to avoid the snowstorm?

   _____

   _____

   _____

   _____

   _____

Daily Dilemma: Thunderstorms

Name _____ Date_____

Today, as you travel across the plains, the heat becomes unbearable. Suddenly, out of nowhere, comes a violent thunderstorm. Discuss the following questions and record your answers in your journals.

1. Who will be more affected by the lightning and thunder, the animals, or the families? Why?

_____

_____

_____

_____

_____

_____

_____

2. What damage might the thunderstorm cause?

_____

_____

_____

_____

_____

_____

_____

Food Supply Chart

Name _____ Date_____

Below and on page 150 you will find a list of food supplies that you will have to have on the trip. Your job will be to estimate the depletion of monthly supplies. Predict what supplies you will need at the next town or trading post.

Food Item	Month					
	1st	2nd	3rd	4th	5th	6th
bacon						
baking soda						
biscuits						
coffee						
cornmeal						
dried beans						
dried fruit						
flatbread						
flour						

Food Supply Chart *(cont.)*

Name _____ Date_____

See page 149 for directions.

Food Item	Month					
	1st	2nd	3rd	4th	5th	6th
ground corn						
lard						
pepper						
rice						
salt						
sugar						
tea						
vinegar						
water						

Friend or Foe?

Students can study the habitats and behavior patterns of animals native to the Western Territory and include their findings in their daily journals. Have students complete the "Friend or Foe?" worksheet and give an oral presentation to class.

Materials

Research Tools:

- reference books
- encyclopedias
- magazines
- novels

Electronic Reference:

- Internet
- *Grollier's Encyclopedia* on CD-ROM

Have the pioneer family groups research animals native to the Western Territory (see page 152).

The students should include in their research the habitats of the animals, and their behaviors towards humans, and complete the "Friend or Foe" worksheet.

Encourage the students to draw pictures, diagrams, and act out the animals' behaviors, including the sounds they make. Have students imagine interesting and exciting ways to present their research findings to the class.

Friend or Foe? *(cont.)*

Name _____ Date_____

Below is a list of many animals native to the Western Territory. Most of the animals will be the ones that you will encounter along your journey. To research these animals, you can use reference books, encyclopedias, magazines, or novels as well as electronic reference materials such as the Internet or *Grollier's Encyclopedias* on CD-ROM. After your research, please complete the attached worksheet and prepare to present an oral report to the class, using posters, diagrams, drawings, skits, or other presentation tools. Use the spaces provided for notes you may wish to take as you complete your research.

antelope	beaver	black bear
buffalo	**coyote**	**elk**
grizzly bear	**prairie dog**	**wolf**

Friend or Foe Worksheet

Name _____ Date_____

Based on the information you have gathered during the Westward Expansion unit, fill in the following worksheet to show whether the following animals are friends or foes.

Animal	Habitat	Friend or Foe to Pioneers	Pioneers' Use of the Animal (food, work, clothing, etc.)
antelope			
beaver			
black bear			
buffalo			
coyote			
elk			
grizzly bear			
prairie dog			
wolf			

Vocabulary Log

Name _____ Date_____

Keep a vocabulary log of new words that you learn throughout the westward expansion unit. You can write definitions and use the words in sentences or write stories based on your adventures. You may also draw illustrations to help you remember the meanings of the words.

anesthetics	moccasin
axle	mountain man
bowie knife	pioneers
buffalo chips	Plains Indians
bull boat	pony express
cholera	prickly pear
draft animals	propaganda
dysentery	rabies
flatboat	sage plant
ford	squaw
groundwater	telegraph
gully	teepee
hardwood	winch
jack	

Westward Expansion Weather Chart

Have students chart the weather conditions along the westward expansion trail during their trip and make predictions based on the weather patterns. (Reproduce the chart at the bottom of this page or have students create their own.) Students can include their completed weather charts in their journals or on the computer and present them to the class.

Materials

- *Farmer's Almanac*
- oaktag or poster board
- markers
- chart paper or butcher paper
- rulers

Have students meet into their pioneer family groups to discuss the weather conditions on their trip.

Each pioneer family group will use a *Farmer's Almanac* to study the weather patterns and predictions.

Students will design a chart predicting the weather that the pioneers will likely encounter on their westward expansion trip.

Students will draw conclusions and make adjustments in their plans according to the weather predictions.

Date	Location	Weather	Prediction

Westward Expansion Map

Have students create a scaled map of their westward journey as they map out their routes. They may create a map on the computer, using a paint, draw, or graphics software program. Students can share their maps with the class.

Materials

Reference Tools:

- atlas
- chart paper
- pencil
- pens
- large piece of oaktag or poster board
- ruler
- markers

Technology:

- paint, draw, or graphics software program

Each family will be given a different trail to follow as well as a different starting point.

Each group of students will research the trails and map out their own route on chart paper or oaktag poster board.

Groups of students will present their maps to the class.

Have students compare a map of the west from the 1800s to a current map. (See page 167 for maps.)

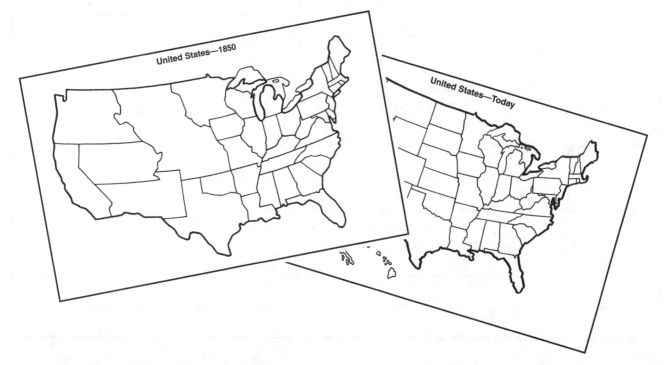

Research on Native American Tribes

Have students develop research skills to access and retrieve information about Native American Indian tribes found in the old West. Students can write and illustrate a report by using a word processor and other graphic software programs. Observe the students as they gather information and prepare their class presentations.

Materials

Reference Tools:

- historical reference materials
- children's literature, *Knots on a Counting Rope* (See bibliography, page 240.)

Technology—Internet Web Sites:

- Native American Home Page- (http://galaxy.einet.net/galaxy/Community/Culture/Native-American.html)
- National Museum of the American Indian Home Page (http://www.si.edu/nmai)
- *Oregon Trail* software program

Read the children's literature selection, *Knots on a Counting Rope* by Bill Martin Jr. and John Archambault, to the class and discuss the importance of storytelling in the Native American culture.

Each pioneer family group will research a Native American Indian tribe that was native to the area they crossed on their journey.

After extensive research of their assigned tribes, the students will answer questions concerning the relationships of their tribes with the pioneers.

Students can use the Internet to access and retrieve information.

Students can also use the *Oregon Trail* software program, which will address the diversity of learning styles of your students.

Have students write a script of a scene from a play in which pioneers discuss with Native American issues about traveling through their lands.

Students can act out this scene in front of the class. A videotape of this scene can be made for future activities.

Students can write a story that depicts an aspect of the history or culture of the particular tribe they research.

Research on Native American Tribes *(cont.)*

Content DR-TA (Directed Reading-Thinking Activity)

- Before reading, have students predict what the story will be about based on the title, the cover of the book, and their background knowledge. Students can work with partners or in small groups to brainstorm ideas and list in their learning logs everything they know about Native American Indians.

- The teacher announces the specific topic, courage and naming ceremonies. Have students go back and check off the items on their lists that relate to "courage and naming ceremonies."

- Ask students to add new ideas to their lists that directly relate to " courage and naming ceremonies."

- Read, *Knots on a Counting Rope* by B. Martin and J. Archambault. Have students evaluate their predictions by circling the correct items they have on their lists. Students can make new predictions before they read the next page.

- As a whole class, discuss predictions and outcomes and specific knowledge that was learned in *Knots on a Counting Rope*.

Directed Inquiry Activity on Heroes of the Wild West

Name _____ Date_____

Before you read the following text selections, "Wild Bill Hickok," "Bill Pickett," and "Annie Oakley," make predictions by answering the questions below. Record your responses on the spaces provided. Add your completed page to your learning log.

- Why do you think cowboys moved to the Wild West?

  _____

  _____

  _____

- How did a person become a hero of the Wild West?

  _____

  _____

  _____

- What were some of the difficulties of being a marshal of a lawless town?

  _____

  _____

  _____

- What were some employment opportunities in the West during the 1800's?

  _____

  _____

  _____

- Were there any women heroines of the Wild West?

  _____

  _____

  _____

- After you read the selection, go back and revise your responses and predictions. Share your responses with your partner or in small groups.

  _____

  _____

  _____

- Create a semantic map representing the complex relationships among the main ideas, concepts, and scientific information from these text selections.

"Wild Bill Hickok" and "Bill Pickett" and "Annie Oakley"

Wild Bill Hickok

Wild Bill Hickok represents the heroes who tamed the rough and rugged West. He was born with the name James Butler Hickok in Troy Grove, Illinois, in 1837. He was the son of a Presbyterian deacon. When he was 18 years old, he moved to Kansas. While there, he worked as a farmer and was a soldier in the Free State Army, which was active in the antislavery movement. In 1858, he started working as a constable for the city of Monticello. One year later, he became a teamster for a Sante Fe freight caravan. Later, he took a job as a stagecoach driver on the Oregon and Sante Fe trails.

In 1861, Hickok was attacked by a bear. He moved to Rock Creek, Nebraska, in order to recover from his wounds. While living in Rock Creek, he got into a dispute with some settlers. He killed three of them and was tried for murder. The shooting was ruled self-defense and he was freed. Later that same year, Hickok helped the Union's Civil War effort by taking charge of a wagon train that took supplies from Fort Leavenworth, Kansas, to Sedalia, Missouri. After that, he worked as a Union scout and guerrilla fighter for the remainder of the war.

Hickok had a reputation for being a marksman. So, in 1869, he was hired as the marshal of Hays City, in Kansas. Three years later, he was the marshal of Abilene, a cattle town in Kansas. He brought law and order to these wild frontier towns. As a result, he became famous for his courage and sense of fairness.

In 1872, Hickok went east with Buffalo Bill's Wild West Show. Two years later he went to Cheyenne, Wyoming, to marry Agnes Lake. In 1876, Hickok met an untimely death when he was shot in the back by Jack McCall during a poker game. McCall was tried, convicted, and hanged for Wild Bill Hickok's murder.

""Wild Bill Hickok" and "Bill Pickett" and "Annie Oakley" *(cont.)*

Bill Pickett

Bill Pickett was born near Liberty Hill, Texas, which is located on the South San Gabriel River. His exact date of birth is not known, but most historians believe it was sometime between 1860 and 1870. He was the son of Thomas and Virginia Jefferson. Pickett's mother was a Choctaw Indian. His father was reported as being part African American, Caucasian, and Native American.

After completing the fifth grade, Pickett took a variety of odd jobs in towns, such as Georgetown, Taylor, Florence, and Round Rock. Then he started working on the Garrett King Ranch. He was a range rider and helped tame wild horses and mules. One day, Pickett was trying to load a steer onto a stock car in Taylor. The steer tried to run away. Pickett grabbed the steer's horns, turned its head, bit it on the lip, and wrestled it down to the ground. This was so effective that Pickett used it as a stunt in the rodeo. Audiences were very impressed, and Pickett became a star.

Shortly after the turn of the century, Zack, Joe, and George Miller were organizing the Miller Brothers 101 Wild West Show. They invited Pickett to perform his "bulldogging" stunt as part of their show. Audiences enthusiastically watched Pickett as he seemed to fly off of his galloping horse, grab and position the steer, and throw it down to the ground with nothing but his teeth touching the steer.

Pickett worked with the Millers for almost thirty years. He performed his bulldogging stunt for audiences throughout North America and England. He performed with noted celebrities such as Will Rogers and Tom Mix.

Pickett retired in the early part of the 1930s. He purchased land in Oklahoma near Chandler. One day he was stomped by a wild horse while trying to rope it. Pickett died as a result of those injuries on April 2, 1932. Bill Pickett was honored as the first African American cowboy by the Rodeo Hall of the National Cowboy Hall of Fame in 1972.

"Wild Bill Hickok" and "Bill Pickett" and "Annie Oakley" *(cont.)*

Annie Oakley

Annie Oakley was born in 1860 in Darke County, Ohio. Her name at birth was Phoebe Ann Moses. By the age of eight, she had learned to shoot and helped her family by hunting animals for food. Annie became a professional marksman by the time she was 15. She participated in many shooting contests that took place in Cincinnati. She beat Frank Butler in a shooting match, which sparked a romance between them. Annie and Frank were married in 1876. Soon afterwards, Annie started calling herself Annie Oakley. In 1885, Annie joined Buffalo Bill's Wild West Show. She gave a fascinating performance with the assistance of her husband. She would shoot a dime out of his hand or a cigarette out of his mouth. Annie also did a trick during which

her husband, who was standing 90 feet (27 m) away from her, threw a playing card into the air and she shot it. Annie's accuracy amazed audiences. She was often called "Little Sure Shot," a nickname that was given to her by Sitting Bull, a Sioux Indian chief.

Annie's performances were extremely popular. She went on tour in Europe and did shows for a variety of people, including the Queen of England and the German Crown Prince Wilhelm. Unfortunately, in 1901, Annie was seriously injured in a train accident. As a result of her injuries, she had to resign her position with Buffalo Bill's Wild West Show. However, after she recovered she started working with a theatrical group. In 1902, Annie starred in *The Western Girl*. In 1914, World War I broke out. For the duration of the war (1914–1918), Annie worked with American soldiers to show them how to shoot. Annie died on November 3, 1926.

Beginning Researcher—Becoming a Sociologist

Name _____ Date_____

You are a sociologist, a person who studies groups of people, specializing in Native American Indian tribes located in the western part of North America during the westward expansion era. Your research project is to study the tribes and explore their history and culture. You may want to specifically study their religious rituals and ceremonies, their leadership, and the language patterns used by the tribe members. You need to find out where the tribe was located, how they hunted, what kind of food they ate, and the symbolism represented through their ceremonies. In your research you may want to compare the Native American tribes you are researching to another tribe a colleague is researching, or you may want to collaborate with a partner. You may gather journal articles, photographs, or other artifacts throughout your research. On your westward journey take your own photographs, or draw illustrations, and collect authentic artifacts for further research. Keep a journal to record notes, comments, and questions that require further inquiry. Present your research findings to your class as a way to honor the Native American people. Use the space below to write your beginning research ideas.

Phase One: The teacher reads a section of related text to the class, and you take notes and develop research ideas.

_____

_____

_____

_____

Phase Two: Make a list of appropriate sources (primary and secondary) you should read and then take notes. Write down questions that need further investigation.

_____

_____

_____

_____

Phase Three: Initiate and carry out research (for example, visit the library or appropriate Internet sites).

_____

_____

_____

_____

Native American Tribes

Name _____ Date_____

Choose one of the following Native American Indian tribes below to research. Write a story that depicts an aspect of their history or culture.

BLACKFOOT	**OTOE**
PAIUTE	**IROQUOIS**
SIOUX	**ARAPAHO**
PAWNEE	
CROW	
MANDAN	
WINNEBAGO	
NAVAJO	

Sociologist's Journal

Name _____ Date_____

Which Native American tribes did you meet on your westward journey?

_____

_____

_____

_____

What did you learn from the Native American Indians you met?

_____

_____

_____

_____

How did the Native American Indians contribute to your journey?

_____

_____

_____

_____

Describe your first meeting with the Native American Indians.

_____

_____

_____

_____

What did you teach them?

_____

_____

_____

_____

What did the Native Americans contribute to the North American culture?

_____

_____

_____

_____

Then and Now

After researching and learning more about the Native American Indians during the westward expansion era, have students compare the Native American Indians then and now. Discuss the issues of stereotyping Native Americans in the movies and on television, the media portrayal, and the relationship between the Native American Indians and the American government.

- Students can create a semantic map displaying the important concepts, ideas, treaties, tribes, leaders, and so on that contributed to the current status of Native American culture.

- Students can create a time line to plot important dates and treaties that explain the relationship with the American government.

- Students can generate ideas for scripts for role playing scenes of the historical confrontations between the Native American Indians and the white man.

- Students can compare geographical maps that show the territories owned by the Native Americans in the mid-1800s and currently.

**Native American Tribes
in the United States**

Then and Now *(cont.)*

United States—1850

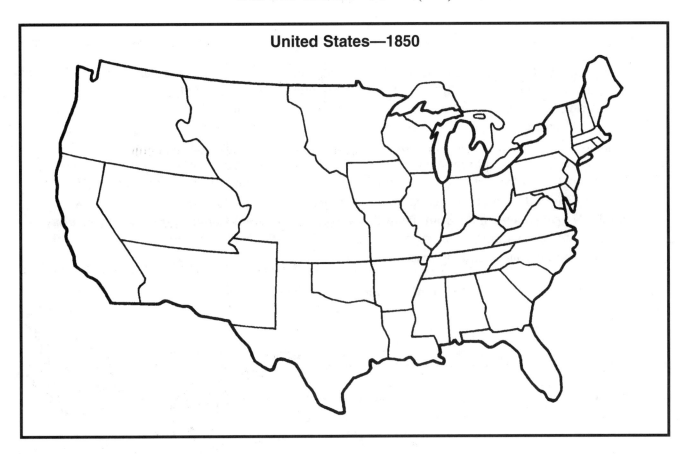

United States—Today

Becoming a Native American Art Historian

Name _____ Date_____

You are an art historian for the local museum of art, specializing in Native American art from the tribes located in the western part of North America. Your research project is to study the symbols and patterns portrayed in their artistic masterpieces. Many Native Americans sell their crafts at trading posts and powwows, which are tribal ceremonies. Explain how they use their art as a way to maintain and honor their history and culture. You may want to specifically study their religious rituals and ceremonies, which require appropriate costumes and face painting. You may gather photos from magazine articles and other artifacts throughout your research or search the Internet to download graphics and images that can be included in your research report. In your research you may want to compare the Native American art from the mid-1800s to the Native American art of the present day. Present your research findings in an art fair as a way to honor the Native American people. Use the space below to write your beginning research ideas.

Phase One: The teacher reads a section of related text to the class, and you take notes and develop research ideas.

_____

_____

_____

_____

Phase Two: Make a list of appropriate sources (primary and secondary) you should read and then take notes. Write down questions that need further investigation.

_____

_____

_____

_____

Phase Three: Initiate and carry out research (for example, visit the library or appropriate Internet sites).

_____

_____

_____

_____

Art Historian's Notebook

Name _____ Date _____

Art Item:

Symbolism:

Design:

Artist:

Tribe:

Year:

Art Item:

Symbolism:

Design:

Artist:

Tribe:

Year:

Art Item:

Symbolism:

Design:

Artist:

Tribe:

Year:

Art Item:

Symbolism:

Design:

Artist:

Tribe:

Year:

World War II

A World War II unit can be very comprehensive and can easily integrate all content areas. The information available on this war is extensive; therefore, you need to determine which aspects of the war—social, economic, political, or historical aspects—are most appropriate for this unit of study. A variety of reading and writing strategies can be used within this unit to help students access, retrieve, and organize information. Students will be encouraged to collect and gather information as well as assume the role of a prisoner of war or an adult who is able to help others escape being sent to concentration camps. As students study the historical events of World War II, they will become actively involved in their learning and live through the experience in a variety of strategies and lessons. These lessons should be adapted to meet the curriculum and individual needs of your class.

Included in this unit of study about World War II are individual activities as well as small group and whole-class activities. Activities are also provided that integrate the curriculum areas of social science, mathematics, art, music, reading, writing, and research skills.

K-W-L Plus Worksheet

Name _____ Date_____

Use this K-W-L Plus worksheet during a class discussion to brainstorm what your students know and what they want to know about World War II, Adolf Hitler, and Nazi Germany. The third column will be completed at the end of the unit as part of a culminating activity. Here are some topics to consider as you begin your worksheet.

- Adolf Hitler
- Holocaust
- Anne Frank
- atom bomb
- relocation

For this activity you will also break into groups and create concept maps, using the information they already know. As the unit continues, students will fill in new information.

K What I Know	W What I Want to Know	L What I Learned

World War II Concept Map

Name _____ Date_____

Based on what you already know about World War II, fill in the concept map. You may add extra boxes if you want to. Work with partners to fill in more information from the K-W-L Plus worksheet. On the next page explain the relationships between the main concept and the other ideas and concepts you have added to the web.

World War II Relationships

Name _____ Date_____

Use this page to explain the relationships among the main concept, World War II, and the other ideas and concepts you have added to your concept web. Be sure to make the connection and the integration clear so that as you add more information, you do not become confused.

My ideas are connected to the main concept of World War II in the following ways:

_____

_____

_____

_____

_____

_____

_____

_____

_____

_____

_____

_____

_____

_____

_____

Teaching WWII Vocabulary in Context

There are many specific vocabulary words you might want to teach during this unit of study. Here are a few suggestions to begin teaching vocabulary in context. Display the words and sentences on a chart so your students can refer to them and recognize the context clues as they read the text selection, "A Short History of Nazi Germany."

- Read the sentence aloud to your class and have your students guess what they think the word means.

- Record the students' guesses and ideas on the chart.

- Agree on a definition by checking in a dictionary or glossary if necessary.

Allies

When Germany was defeated by a combination of allies, including England, France, Italy, and the United States, in World War I, it proclaimed itself a republic and sued for peace.

Treaty

The Allies forced Germany to sign the Treaty of Versailles, inflicting huge penalties on the beaten country.

Indignation

The anger and indignation the German people felt did not lessen as time went on, and the economic results of the treaty included upwardly spiraling inflation, taking much of what they needed for their daily needs.

Nationalistic

The feeling their country had been "stabbed in the back" grew through the 1920s and gave rise to various nationalistic groups.

Aryan

He said that "real" Germans were the members of a superior Aryan race and that the Jews, Gypsies, and the Slavs of Eastern Europe were subhuman, not fit to live in civilized society.

World War II: Question-Answer Relationships

A Short History of Nazi Germany

In 1900, Germany, a very large country compared to most of its tiny European neighbors, was Europe's strongest power. When it was defeated by a combination of allies, including England, France, Italy, and the United States, in World War I, it proclaimed itself a republic and sued for peace. The German leaders hoped to help frame the Treaty of Versailles which ended the war, but all the victorious Allies except the United States were determined to punish the new republic.

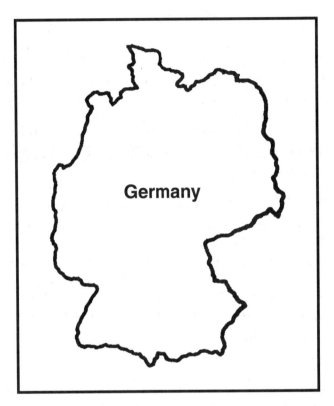

The Allies forced Germany to sign the Treaty of Versailles, inflicting huge penalties on the beaten country. The treaty placed full blame for the war on Germany and stripped it of its territories. Germany was disarmed and ordered to pay huge amounts for the damages it had done to civilian properties in all of Europe. The punishment was more than most Germans would accept. Not only were they impoverished by the terms of the treaty but the proud people were also severely humiliated.

The anger and indignation the German people felt did not lessen as time went on and the economic results of the treaty included upwardly spiraling inflation, taking much of what they needed for their daily needs. Most Germans did not accept blame for the war and felt they were being unfairly singled out as the cause of a war which had multiple causes. The feeling their country had been "stabbed in the back" grew through the 1920s and gave rise to various nationalistic groups. One of these groups, the National Socialist German Worker's Party, led by a former house painter named Adolf Hitler, grew as it attracted all sorts of malcontents. They called themselves Nazis.

Hitler's entire life and personality were governed by hate and anger. A gifted orator, he was able to arouse the enthusiasm of huge groups of people. Hitler's message to the German people was that the Jews had caused all of Germany's woes and that they were at fault for Germany's decline in world prestige. He said that "real" Germans were the members of a superior Aryan race and that the Jews, Gypsies, and the Slavs of Eastern Europe were subhuman, not fit to live in civilized society.

Hitler touched an old racist nerve in the German masses as he preached his message of violence and hate, and the racism he encouraged fed on the humiliations of the postwar years. Because the German people longed to once again have their former power and prestige restored, Hitler's party attracted a wide following.

World War II: Question-Answer Relationships *(cont.)*

A Short History of Nazi Germany *(cont.)*

The Nazi Party was one of many small political parties in Germany. In 1932, thirteen years after it began, the Nazis became the largest party in the Reichstag, Germany's legislative body. The aged President von Hindenburg of the Republic was unable to keep control, and in 1933 Hitler convinced the old man to appoint him Chancellor of Germany. Immediately, Hitler demanded that the Reichstag grant him emergency powers for four years. The Reichstag gave in to Hitler's demands and then dissolved itself. Hitler, within two months of becoming Chancellor, became absolute ruler of Germany.

From then on, nothing could stop him. Before he committed suicide twelve years later, fifty-five million people would die in Europe.

Many people did not believe that Hitler would eliminate all those he considered unworthy to live, but most German people accepted his rule. Those who did not turned their heads and closed their eyes as he developed his dreaded secret police, the Gestapo. He turned these Storm Troopers loose on Jews and began the grisly job of erecting places of mass murder and slave labor, the concentration camps. A few Jews left Germany during the early years, but escape soon became impossible for most.

Hitler moved quickly to put his racist theories into practice. Jews were dismissed from government positions and forbidden to work in universities, schools, radio, movies, the theater, or journalism. They were not allowed to practice law or medicine or engage in business. All their means of earning a livelihood were taken from them. Jews were segregated, and Jewish children were forbidden to go to school with non-Jewish children. Non-Jews could not work for Jews or marry them.

In 1939, the army Hitler had been preparing for six years began to roll. Poland fell in eighteen days to Germany. Denmark, Norway, Holland, Belgium, and France were conquered within six months. Hitler had signed a non-aggression treaty with Joseph Stalin, the dictator of the Soviet Union, but it did not stop him from attacking that country, as well. A dark cloud had descended on Europe. For the six years it took the combined forces of England, the United States, Russia, and the underground forces to liberate Europe, Hitler's concentration camps continued as efficient killing machines, and all Europe was devastated. Total evil had been turned on the continent of Europe, an evil that would not be defeated until May 1945.

Adolph Hitler   **Joseph Stalin**

World War II: Question-Answer Relationships *(cont.)*

Name _____   Date_____

Directions: Read the selection on pages 178 and 179. Complete the following chart and add this page to your learning log. Share your answers and decisions in a whole-class discussion.

In the Book

In My Head

Right There

On which continent is Germany located?

_____

_____

_____

_____

_____

_____

Author and You

How did Adolph Hitler become absolute ruler of Germany?

_____

_____

_____

_____

_____

_____

_____

Think and Search

What happened to Germany before, after, or during World War II?

_____

_____

_____

_____

_____

On My Own

Explain one of the racist theories held by some people in today's society.

_____

_____

_____

_____

_____

World War II: Question-Answer Relationships *(cont.)*

The Holocaust

The word **holocaust** means total destruction, usually by fire. Since World War II it has earned a new meaning: the massacre of six million Jews by the German Nazis. Hitler's main goal was to exterminate all the Jews in Europe and he succeeded in killing two-thirds of them before ending his own life with poison in his bunker under the German Chancellery building in Berlin.

The Holocaust began as soon as Hitler took power. Between 1933 and 1939 the Nazis boycotted Jewish businesses, established quotas in the professions and schools, outlawed marriages between Jews and Gentiles, and built Dachau, Buchenwald, and Oranienburg, the first concentration camps. On the night of November 9, 1938, Hitler's Storm Troopers went on a rampage, burning 267 synagogues, arresting 20,000 people, and smashing Jewish places of business in an orgy of terror which has since been called **Kristallnacht,** "the night of broken glass." To make a horrible night worse, the Nazis then forced the Jews to pay an "atonement" fine of $400 million for the damage which had been done by the government to the Jews' own property.

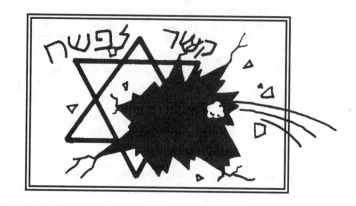

World War II began for Europe in September 1939. (The United States did not enter the war until December 1941.) After Germany conquered Poland, Reinhard Heydrich decreed that all Polish Jews were to be confined in a **ghetto.** Seven hundred thousand of them died during the next two years, and when Germany attacked the Soviet Union in June 1941, "strike squads" were sent in against Soviet Jewish citizens. On September 29, 1941, in one atrocity alone, 33,771 Jews were machine-gunned.

In January 1942, Hitler called the **Wannsee Conference** to debate what he called the "final solution of the Jewish question." As a result, during the next three years Jews represented over half of those exterminated in the concentration camps. Gypsies, Slavs, and political prisoners made up most of the rest. Several camps, including **Auschwitz**, were actually extermination camps built to kill people. The Nazis were proud of their efficiency in murder, and their methods included cyanide, carbon monoxide gas, electrocution, and phenol injections.

The concentration camps have come to stand for the worst that humans can do. They totally debased and depersonalized the inmates, treating them as though they were not people at all, crowding them onto cattle cars, as many as a hundred to a car, and carrying them to the camps without water, food, or sanitary facilities. They abused them physically and verbally in the worst ways possible and split up families, sending men and boys to one place and women and girls to another. In **Auschwitz** the infamous medical director, Dr. Mengele, decided, with one look at the incoming prisoners, which ones would live and which would die.

World War II: Question-Answer Relationships *(cont.)*

The Holocaust *(cont.)*

Everything prisoners owned—money, clothing, books, jewelry, even the hair on their heads and the gold fillings in their teeth—was taken from them. They slept on wooden shelves which served as beds, crowded so closely together they could not turn over in their sleep. There were no blankets or pillows.

They were forced to work as slave laborers until they could no longer work, and then they were killed. The prisoners were called by the numbers tattooed on their arms. Hundreds of thousands died of typhus or other terrible diseases which flourish when people are forced to live together in unsanitary conditions. Thousands of whole families were wiped out.

Having no weapons and weakened by disease and malnutrition, the Jews were isolated from the Allies with little resource except to hide, as the Franks did for two years. Escape was impossible after the early years. Sixty thousand managed to join up with partisan groups who fiercely resisted the Nazis throughout the war, and uprisings occurred in several of the larger ghettos, including the one in Warsaw, Poland.

Those killed included men, women, children, babies, old people, and the handicapped. They included doctors, teachers, librarians, lawyers, business people, store clerks, housewives, students, farmers, and secretaries. People from every walk of life were killed, regardless of who they were, how wealthy or how poor they were, or how good or how bad they were. They were all the same to the misfits and criminals who ran the government and the camps.

The camp to which Anne Frank, her mother, and her sister were taken first was Auschwitz in Poland, the largest of the camps and considered a model extermination camp. Its gas chambers were large enough to kill hundreds of people at once and its huge furnaces burned the bodies of the dead. Columns of black smoke rose from the furnaces into the air twenty-four hours a day. Anne's mother died there, and then Anne and Margot were taken to **Bergen-Belsen**. In Auschwitz there was a little food to eat, but in Belsen there was nothing. It was only a matter of time until Margot, and then Anne, died of typhus.

The holocaust is one of the darkest chapters in all of human history. It was truly a time when the inmates ran the show, when evil was turned loose on the inhabitants of a whole continent and became official policy.

WW II Reading Response Groups

The following prompts will guide you in the discussion of Nazi Germany. Read the text selection, "A Short History of Nazi Germany." In a group, discuss the social, economic, and political effects of the Nazi party and the Nazi invasions. Share your group's responses with the whole class after you have had time to meet in small groups. Use the space provided to write your own ideas.

1. What was the economic climate of Germany at the time of Hitler's rise to power?

   _____

   _____

   _____

   _____

2. How did the requirements of the Treaty of Versailles affect Germany?

   _____

   _____

   _____

   _____

3. What might have happened if there had been widespread public demonstrations against Hitler's beliefs and policies?

   _____

   _____

   _____

   _____

4. What are the dangers of anti-Semitism?

   _____

   _____

   _____

   _____

WW II Word Sleuths

Name _____ Date_____

Imagine you are a word sleuth investigating the origins and meanings of words, terms, phrases, word families, and concepts. Collect the words from the various text selections about WW II, novels such as *Anne Frank: Diary of a Young Girl,* or *Farewell to Manzanar* and your own historical research. Record your words and investigative findings in your vocabulary log or your learning log. Be sure to look for words borrowed from other languages and cultures.

Word	Origin	Meaning

Anne Frank: The Diary of a Young Girl

Have students read the novel, *Anne Frank: The Diary of a Young Girl* (Frank, 1967), during the World War II unit. This poignant story is about a young Jewish girl in Amersterdam, Holland, who was hiding from the threat of becoming a prisoner in a concentration camp. This story will help students learn more about World War II through the eyes of a child. Information learned from the novel can be included in concept maps, the K-W-L worksheet and the many other activities in this unit.

Content DR-TA (Directed Reading-Thinking Activity)

Before reading, have students predict what the story will be about based on the title and the cover of the book and their background knowledge. Students can work with partners or in small groups to brainstorm ideas and list everything they know about WWII in their learning logs.

- Announce the specific topic, Nazi invasions. Have students go back and check off the items on their lists that relate to "Nazi invasions."

- Ask students to add new ideas to their lists that directly relate to "Nazi invasions."

- After students read each chapter, have them evaluate their predictions by circling the correct items they have on their lists. Students can make new predictions before they continue to read the next chapter.

- As a whole class, discuss predictions, outcomes, and specific knowledge that was learned through the novel.

Double-Entry Journal Prompts

Use the following prompts or create your own for double-entry journals. Have students write their ideas, thoughts, questions, and answers in their journals.

What does the word "war" mean to you? Why might a war be declared?

Explain why this war was called World War II. Describe some of the social, economic, and political outcomes of this war.

Have you ever experienced racial, religious, or ethnic prejudice and discrimination?

How might you cope with this prejudice and discrimination?

Why do people continue to fight religious wars?

Where are religious wars being fought today?

Diary Details

1. For this activity, students will keep diaries as Anne Frank did. Have a class discussion about WWII and why a girl might keep a diary.

2. Discuss two novels about war as seen through the eyes of a child, *Anne Frank: The Diary of a Young Girl,* and *Zlata's Diary: A Child's Life in Sarajevo.* Both of these books, accounts of survival under extremely dangerous wartime conditions, are written in a diary format.

3. Discuss the value of a diary or journal. Have students keep a diary for a week and then compare their entries with Anne Frank's entries or Zlata Filipovic's entries. Have students draw the settings of both stories, based on the authors' descriptions.

4. Have students imagine that there is an invasion of their hometown and they have to go into hiding. Each student should keep a diary for a week while in hiding. Students should include responses to the following questions:

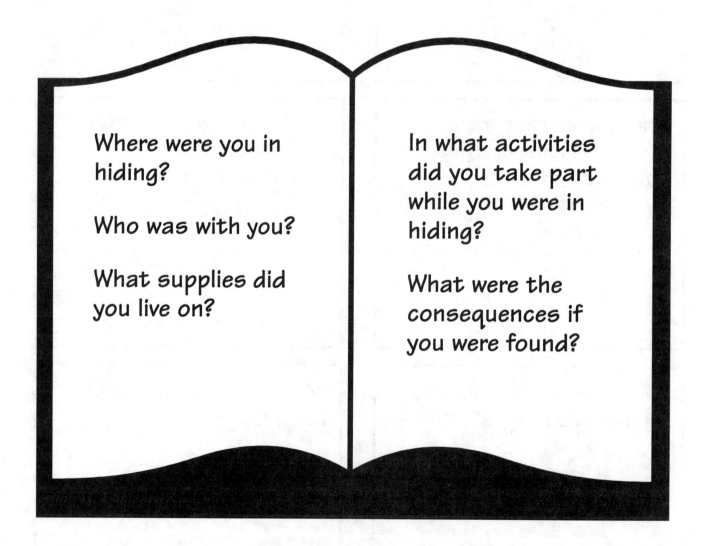

Where were you in hiding?

Who was with you?

What supplies did you live on?

In what activities did you take part while you were in hiding?

What were the consequences if you were found?

Guided Writing

Name _____ Date_____

On the lines provided, write your thoughts, ideas, and answers to the following prompts. Add this page to your journal notebook or folder.

- Imagine you are held a prisoner in a concentration camp (for example, Dachau or Auschwitz). Write a letter to your best friend, explaining what is happening to you.

  _____

  _____

  _____

  _____

- Your entire family has been taken prisoners in concentration camps except for you. How do you survive without them? How do you attempt to free them from the concentration camps? Who do you turn to for help?

  _____

  _____

  _____

  _____

- You have the ability to help others escape being taken as prisoners by hiding them. Where do you hide them? How do you keep them hidden for one month? Explain why you are not taken prisoner.

  _____

  _____

  _____

  _____

- You are a reporter sent over to Germany to cover this war. What aspect of the war might you choose to focus on for your articles? How will you get your information?

  _____

  _____

  _____

  _____

World War II Vocabulary

In pairs or small groups, students nominate one or two words or terms that they believe the class should learn or know more about. The teacher also nominates one or two words, also. Have students keep a vocabulary log of new words they learn throughout the WW II unit. The following words can be used to initiate the vocabulary self-collection process.

Nazi	invasion	hunger
concentration camp	religious persecution	Holocaust
traitor	survival	hope
despair	swastika	atom bomb

Nazi Invasion Routes

Name _____

Date _____

The Nazis invaded many towns and countries in obeying the dictates of their leader, Adolph Hitler. Mark the routes of the Nazi soldiers as they entered towns and villages throughout Europe and loaded the people into trucks for "relocation" to concentration camps. Use this geographical map below to record the invasion routes of the Germans during World War II. Also include the locations of the concentration camps.

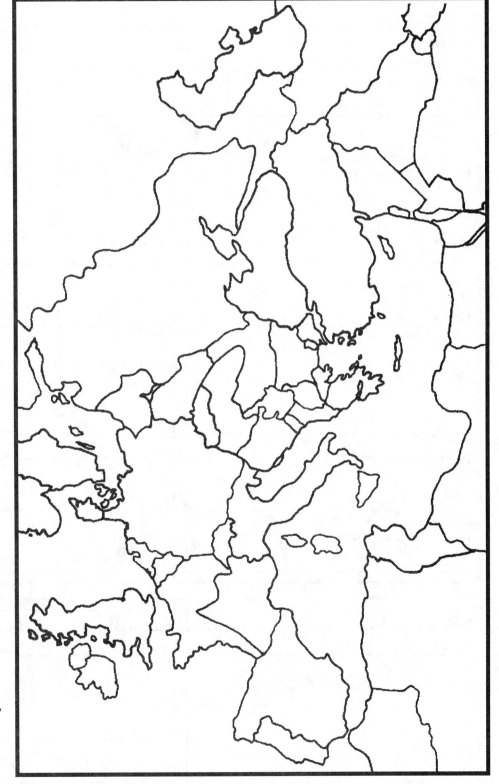

Historical Time Line

Name _____ Date _____

Based on the information you have gathered in your research of WW II, create a historical time line from December 1941 through May 1945. Include important dates, people, and places. You can first write the information on index cards and then place them in the correct chronological order. You may use a computer software program, as well, to organize the information and present it in a time line.

Signs and Symbols

Name _____ Date_____

In the first box below, draw a sign or symbol from World War II and write what the sign or symbol represents. You may include signs or symbols of people, leaders, groups of people, places, religions, and so on. In the second box, create a symbol for yourself.

Symbol from World War II   Description

_____

_____

_____

_____

_____

_____

_____

_____

Symbol for Myself   Description

_____

_____

_____

_____

_____

_____

_____

_____

Semantic Feature Analysis of Movie and Novel

After viewing a movie about Anne Frank, compare the book to the movie, using a semantic feature analysis. Think about the feelings and emotions of the characters depicted in the novel. Some characters may hide their feelings or display different feelings in the movie than in the novel. Complete the semantic feature analysis below. On the left side, vertically list the feelings and emotions of three characters. On the top row, horizontally list the names of the characters. Fill in the chart by placing a positive (+) sign in the box that appropriately describes a character and a negative (–) sign in a box that does not match the feelings and emotions with the character. Do this for both charts, using the same characters for each analysis.

Movie

Novel

Beginning Researcher

Name _____ Date_____

Becoming a World War II Historian

You are an historian for a museum, and your assignment is to research World War II and gather interesting facts about the war to put on display in the museum. You may gather letters, newspaper articles, photographs, personal interviews, or other artifacts throughout your research. Choose a specific topic to research (for example, a person, a geographical location, or invasion routes) and present your research findings to your class. Use the space below to write ideas on how you want to begin each phase of your research.

Phase One: Take notes and develop research ideas while the teacher reads a section of related text.

_____

_____

_____

_____

_____

Phase Two: Make a list of appropriate sources (primary and secondary) you should read and then take notes. Write down questions that need further investigation.

_____

_____

_____

_____

_____

Phase Three: Initiate and carry out research (for example, visit the library or interview appropriate people).

_____

_____

_____

_____

_____

World War II Research Ideas

Name _____ Date_____

Choose one of the topics below for your historical research project.

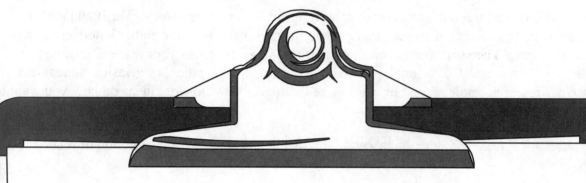

Holocaust	V-2 Rocket
Invasion of Europe	Werner von Braun
Anti-Semitism	The Iron Curtain
Warsaw Ghetto	Mussolini
America in World War II	Queen Elizabeth II
German Occupation of Poland	French Underground
German Occupation of Holland	Terezin Ghetto
The USSR-Germany Non-aggression Pact	The United Nations
	Jerusalem
Winston Churchill	Fascism
Adolph Hitler	Zionism
Albert Einstein	Berlin
Treaty of Versailles	Weimar Republick
Racism	Luftwaffe
Concentration Camps	Food Rationing
Judaism	English Aircraft
Jewish Holidays	Conference at Malta
The Nuremberg Trials	Royal Air Force
Battle of Britain	Christianity
German Occupation of France	Japanese Relocation
German Occupation of Denmark	Pearl Harbor

World War II Historian Notebook

Name _____ Date_____

Use this notebook page to write down notes, questions, answers, comments, or other interesting information you might need while conducting your research. Be sure to include your references, the title and author of books or articles you read, or the names of movies or pictures that contribute to your research. If you interview a person, remember to write down all of his or her personal information, including name, age, birthplace, location of the interview, and so forth.

Directed Inquiry Activity

Name _____ Date_____

Before you read the following text selection, "The Holocaust," make predictions, record your responses below, and include this paper in your learning logs.

- Why do you think it is important to study and analyze historical tragedies?

  _____

  _____

  _____

  _____

  _____

  _____

  _____

- What might happen if a political group took control over your weak government?

  _____

  _____

  _____

  _____

  _____

  _____

  _____

- What other groups of people are suffering from oppression or persecution, such as civil war, economic unrest, or racism?

  _____

  _____

  _____

  _____

  _____

  _____

- After you read the selection, go back and revise your responses and predictions. Share your responses with your partner or in small groups.

- Create a semantic map representing the complex relationships among the main ideas, concepts, and historical information from this text selection.

The Holocaust

The Holocaust is defined as the mass murder of European Jews during World War II by Adolf Hitler's Nazi soldiers. A brief synopsis of the events leading up to and including the Holocaust begins below and concludes on page 196. This summary may be used as a teaching aid or as a guide for discussion. Several classroom activities that address the events of the Holocaust follow this summary. It is important to be as forthright as possible with students when discussing this complex issue. Explain that it is important to study and analyze the dark, somber periods in history so that tragedies such as the Holocaust will never happen again.

Adolf Hitler's Plan to Conquer the World

At the end of World War I, the Allies forced the Central Powers to sign the Treaty of Versailles. This treaty said that Germany was guilty of starting the war and therefore must be punished. The treaty took away one-tenth of the German land. It restricted Germans from building up their military or manufacturing large weapons. The treaty also forced them to pay the Allies large sums of money to reimburse those countries for expenses incurred during the war. It left Germany a poor country with many Germans feeling betrayed by their new democratic government for signing the treaty. Adolf Hitler, who was the head of the Nazi Party (National Socialist German Worker's Party), easily took control over the weak government.

Hitler told the German people that Germany's problems were caused by the Treaty of Versailles and by the Jewish people. The Jews became an easy scapegoat since many people believed that they were to blame for the death of Jesus. Therefore, Hitler decided the solution to Germany's problems was to get more land and to get rid of the Jews. Because so many Germans felt desperate, Hitler soon had a large following.

As Hitler's power and support grew, he began building an army and preparing for war. Eventually, Hitler joined forces with the Italian dictator, Benito Mussolini. Mussolini was also dissatisfied with the terms of the Treaty of Versailles. Japan later joined Germany and Italy to form the Axis powers. Together they began attacking other countries.

As the Nazis forcibly took control of many European countries, Hitler began to pursue the second phase of his plan—the extermination of the Jews. Not only did Hitler plan to completely wipe out the entire Jewish population but he also targeted other groups such as Gypsies, Poles, Slavs, physically or mentally disabled persons, and anyone who opposed him.

The Nazis built special prisons called concentration camps throughout Europe. Jews were forced to leave their jobs, and Jewish-owned businesses were vandalized. Millions of Jews were eventually sent to concentration or death camps such as Auschwitz, Treblinka, Belzec, and Majdanek. These camps included gas chambers, where thousands of Jews were killed with poison gas and huge furnaces where bodies burned. Some of the camps had factories where the prisoners were literally worked to death. Many of the Jews died from disease, starvation, or torture. Doctors sometimes performed cruel medical experiments on the prisoners. Anyone found to be too sick or old to work was killed in the gas chamber.

The Holocaust *(cont.)*

By the time World War II ended, about 6 million out of an estimated 8.3 million Jews living in German-occupied Europe were killed. Denmark is the only country where Resistance Forces were able to smuggle most of their Jewish population into neutral Sweden to escape the Nazi soldiers.

Most people around the world were unaware of the atrocities that were taking place in the concentration camps. When the war ended, the Allied troops saw firsthand the gruesome sights at these camps. It was then that the rest of the world was forced to face the reality of the Holocaust.

Classroom Activities

An effective method of addressing the subject of the Holocaust is to connect it to a current event or a social studies lesson. Have students locate and summarize current newspaper articles that describe people from around the world who are suffering from oppression or persecution such as civil war, economic unrest, or racism. Allow students to share their summaries and then display them on a bulletin board similar to the one suggested below.

WORLD NEWS UPDATE

"Those who cannot remember the past are condemned to repeat it."
—George Santayana, **Life of Reason**

K-W-L Plus Worksheet

As you study the rain forest, think about the sounds of the animals, the aromas of the plants and flowers, and the feel of moisture in the air. Some lessons in this unit focus on the rare species of animals and plants that live and grow in the rain forest, while others focus on the people and products of the rain forest. Throughout this unit you will utilize a variety of content reading and writing strategies to help you access and retrieve information and then organize it so you can retain the information.

Using a K-W-L Plus worksheet helps you organize the information you already know. During a class discussion, brainstorm what you know and what you want to know about the rain forest, using the K-W-L Plus worksheet below. The third column will be completed at the end of the unit as part of a culminating activity.

K What I Know	W What I Want to Know	L What I Learned

Concept Web

Name _____ Date_____

As an introductory activity to the rain forest unit, create a concept web using the information in the K-W-L Plus Worksheet on page 197. Information can be added onto this concept web throughout the unit. On page 199, explain the relationships between the main concept and the other ideas and concepts you have added to the web.

Rain Forest

Rain Forest Relationships

Name _____ Date_____

Use this page to explain the relationships among the main concept, the rain forest, and the other ideas and concepts you have added to your concept web. Be sure to make the connection and the integration clear, so that as you add more information you do not become confused.

My ideas are connected to the main concept of the rain forest in the following ways:

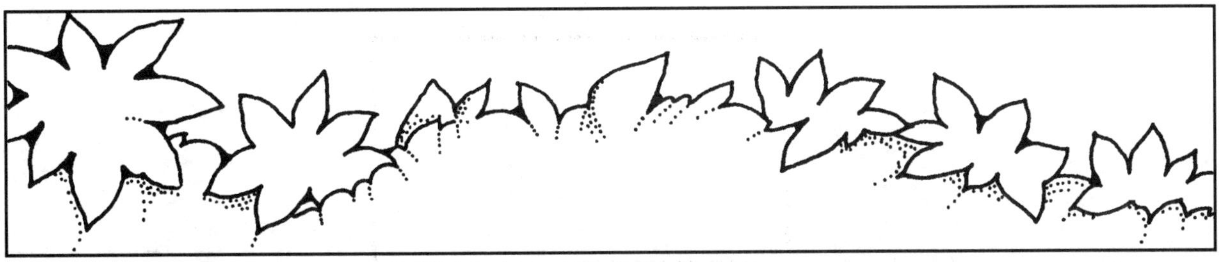

_____

_____

_____

_____

_____

_____

_____

_____

_____

_____

_____

_____

_____

_____

_____

_____

Rain Forest Geographical Map

Name _____ Date_____

Tropical rain forests are located between the Tropics of Cancer and Capricorn where the weather is hot and humid all year long. The yearly rainfall is more than 80 inches, and in some areas it can reach more that 200 inches in one year alone. Temperatures in the tropical rain forests range between 70° and 85° Fahrenheit (21° and 29° Celsius). This type of environment is conducive to an abundance of growth of the rare species of plants that exist nowhere else on earth. Many rare species of animals also live in the tropical rain forests. However, due to ecological problems the rain forests are in danger. With the problems in the ozone layer and global warming, the ecosystem is changing; therefore, it is important to save the rain forests.

In your unit of study on rain forests you will first need to locate the rain forests in the world and identify the animals, plants, and people who live in the unique communities of the tropical rain forests.

Use the following guiding questions in your research on rain forests.

- The equator is found between the Tropic of _____ and the Tropic of _____.

- On which continents can you locate the rain forests?

- Which continents do not have tropical rain forests and why not?

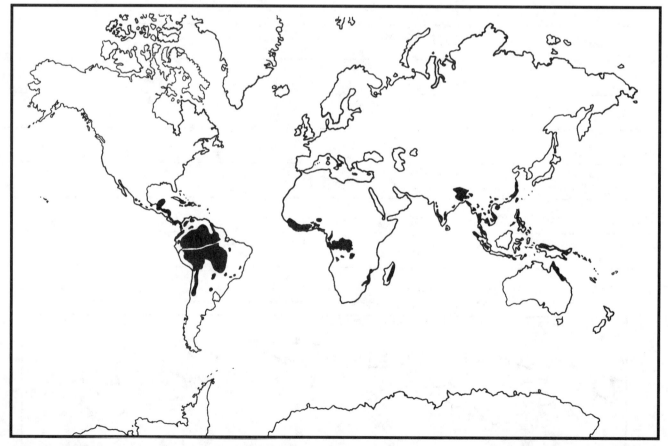

Rain Forest: Question-Answer Relationships

Layers in the Rain Forest

The rain forest is made up of a complex system of layers which includes trees, shrubs, vines, ferns, and other plants. There are no distinct boundaries among the four layers which include the *forest floor, understory, canopy,* and *emergent layer.*

Forest Floor:

The forest floor is carpeted with a soft layer of moss, decaying leaves, and fallen branches. The air in this layer is very still as there is no wind. The thick forest canopy, towering 65 feet (20 meters) above, keeps the forest floor dark even in the daytime. The humidity on the forest floor is always above 70%, making it very muggy. The average rainfall in tropical rain forests is over 80 inches annually, and the temperature remains constant, between $70°$ to $85°$ Fahrenheit ($21°$ to $29°$ Celsius).

The soil in the rain forest is not very fertile. The constant heavy rainfall washes nutrients away quickly before they can be absorbed into the ground. Therefore, root systems are very shallow so they can quickly recycle nutrients.

Ferns, mosses, gingers, and other plants that need very little sunlight grow on the forest floor. Only two percent of the sun's rays filter down to this level. The forest floor is surprisingly free of green vegetation due to the lack of sunlight. Lianas (woody vines) that wind around the forest trees root here.

The animals on this level survive on decomposing dead materials that have fallen from the other levels. There are lots of insects here, including beetles, ants, termites, centipedes, millipedes, and spiders. Also found on the forest floor are worms, rodents, larger mammals, frogs, toads, poisonous snakes (such as the fer-de-lance), armadillos, and caimans (a reptile that looks like an alligator).

Rain Forest: Question-Answer Relationships *(cont.)*

Understory:

Ten to twenty feet (three to six meters) above the forest floor is the understory layer of the rain forest. It is almost as dark here as it is on the forest floor. The humidity is still high here in the understory, and the temperature remains constant.

Small trees and shrubs abound in the understory. The trees at this level have elongated crowns like the flame on a candle. The leaves on the trees are large, enabling them to absorb the diffused sunlight. Some trees will remain at this level their whole lives. Others wait for an opening in the canopy layer created by fallen trees. This opening provides the sunlight and space necessary for the trees to grow to the upper levels.

Fruits and nuts are found growing at this level, which attract many animals. The animals found here cling, leap, swing, and fly from branch to branch. Spider monkeys and tamanduas (anteaters) hang by their tails in this layer. Many animals have adapted to living in the understory. For example, the red-eyed tree frog has special pads on its toes to enable it to cling to trees, flying squirrels have flaps of skin between their toes that help them glide from tree to tree, and anole lizards have long toes with sticky pads which make them good climbers.

Larger mammals (such as jaguars and ocelots) also live at this level where they can find a plentiful supply of small animals for their diets. Many snakes, such as the tree boa and the false coral snake, make their homes here in the understory where they do their hunting at night (which means they are nocturnal). Most insects live here in the understory, becoming part of the food chain for such predators as iguanas, other lizards, snakes, etc.

This abundant supply of insects also feeds the tropical bat population. Each bat can eat up to 3,000 insects per night. Other bats drink nectar from flowers growing here. As the bats drink the nectar in the flowers, they pick up pollen. When they land on their next flower, some of the pollen falls off, thus pollinating the flowers. Still other bats eat tropical fruits. They germinate the rain forest because they eat and eliminate seeds as they fly.

Canopy:

Sixty-five to one hundred feet (20 to 30 meters) high above the forest floor is the canopy, with its flat-topped trees. Here, neither the temperature nor the humidity stays at a constant level. The canopy forms a continuous green covering over the rain forest with its twisting and turning leaves. It acts like a giant umbrella filtering out all but two to five percent of the sunlight and rain.

Rain Forest: Question-Answer Relationships *(cont.)*

The tall trees growing in the canopy layer are supported by a special root system. Some of these trees have round stilt roots while others have buttress roots. The leaves on the trees up here become very wet. Therefore, they have developed special drip tips that allow the water to run off. This keeps their surfaces dry so that molds, lichens, and small plants will not grow on them.

The canopy layer is full of incredibly beautiful plants and flowers like orchids and bromeliads. The bromeliad leaves grow out of its center, forming a bowl. This bowl collects rainwater, thus providing nourishment and a home for salamanders, frogs, birds, and insects.

The canopy layer is like a giant wildlife park. Most of the plants and animals of the rain forest can be found here. There are spider monkeys, sloths, opossums, loud howler monkeys, colorful butterflies, moths, and thousands of birds, including parrots, hummingbirds, paradise tanagers, big-billed toucans, screeching macaws, and oropendolas. Many birds make nests in the hollow trunks of trees to hide from predators. All of these animals call the canopy home.

Emergent:

Towering above the canopy, anywhere between 115 to 150 feet (35 to 46 meters) high, is the emergent layer. One acre of rain forest contains only one or two of these giant trees. Some of these trees can grow up to 250 feet (76 meters) high, like the tualang (TOO-ah-long) of Malaysia. The trees are supported by tall, slender trunks and either thick-ridged buttress roots or circular stilt roots. These trees sport umbrella-shaped crowns.

High above the canopy these towering giants of the rain forest must deal with low humidity, strong winds, and high, changing temperatures. There is constant exposure to the sun's rays. The small, thick, and waxy leaves of these trees are able to retain water in this harsh environment. The small leaves are aerodynamically designed to allow air to move around them.

These skyscrapers of the forest are home to the harpy eagle and morpho butterfly. The few fruits and flowers that are found here take advantage of the winds for pollination and dispersal of their seeds.

Rain Forest: Question-Answer Relationships *(cont.)*

Name _____   Date_____

Directions: Read the selection on pages 201-203. Complete the following chart and add this page to your learning log. Share your answers and decisions in a whole-class discussion.

In the Book   ## In My Head

Right There	**Author and You**
What are the four layers of the rain forest?	If you were an ocelot, in which layer of the rain forest would you live?

Think and Search	**On My Own**
What purpose does the canopy serve in the rain forest?	Compare the layers of the rain forest with the layers of another habitat.

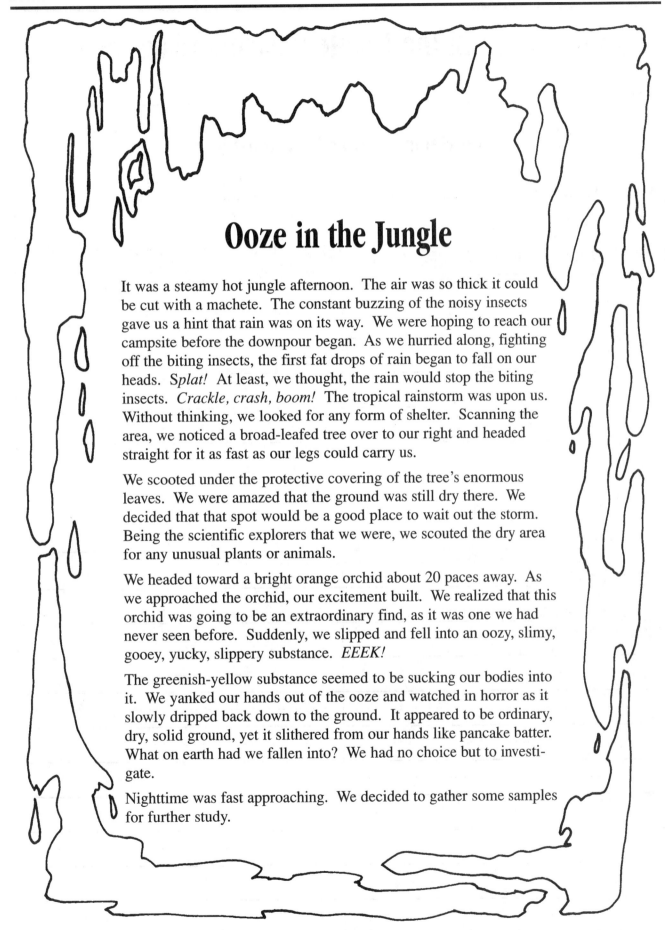

Ooze in the Jungle

It was a steamy hot jungle afternoon. The air was so thick it could be cut with a machete. The constant buzzing of the noisy insects gave us a hint that rain was on its way. We were hoping to reach our campsite before the downpour began. As we hurried along, fighting off the biting insects, the first fat drops of rain began to fall on our heads. *Splat!* At least, we thought, the rain would stop the biting insects. *Crackle, crash, boom!* The tropical rainstorm was upon us. Without thinking, we looked for any form of shelter. Scanning the area, we noticed a broad-leafed tree over to our right and headed straight for it as fast as our legs could carry us.

We scooted under the protective covering of the tree's enormous leaves. We were amazed that the ground was still dry there. We decided that that spot would be a good place to wait out the storm. Being the scientific explorers that we were, we scouted the dry area for any unusual plants or animals.

We headed toward a bright orange orchid about 20 paces away. As we approached the orchid, our excitement built. We realized that this orchid was going to be an extraordinary find, as it was one we had never seen before. Suddenly, we slipped and fell into an oozy, slimy, gooey, yucky, slippery substance. *EEEK!*

The greenish-yellow substance seemed to be sucking our bodies into it. We yanked our hands out of the ooze and watched in horror as it slowly dripped back down to the ground. It appeared to be ordinary, dry, solid ground, yet it slithered from our hands like pancake batter. What on earth had we fallen into? We had no choice but to investigate.

Nighttime was fast approaching. We decided to gather some samples for further study.

Ooze in the Jungle: Learning Log

Name _____ Date_____

Question-Answer Relationships

Title of text selection _____

In the Book QARs

_____

_____

_____

_____

_____

In My Head QARs

_____

_____

_____

_____

_____

_____

_____

_____

_____

_____

Group Mapping Activity

After reading "Layers in the Rain Forest," have students create a map that explains what they believe to be the important concepts and ideas from the text. Students should not talk to classmates or look back at the text. Share the sample map below with students, if necessary.

1. Have students share their maps with a partner or members in a small group.

> Remind students to explain the following:
> - what they chose to include
> - how they chose to design their maps
> - why they made their specific choices

2. Have students work collaboratively with partners or in small groups to finish their maps.

3. Encourage students to review the text to clarify questions or information.

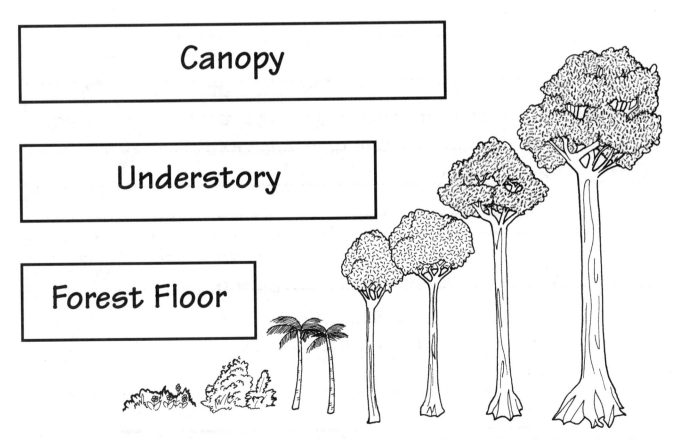

Emergent

Canopy

Understory

Forest Floor

Rain Forest Reading Response Groups

Use the following sample prompts to guide students in the discussion of animals that inhabit the rain forest. Create additional prompts for some or all of the remaining animal cards. Students can read the, "Animal Information Cards" on pages 209–217 and discuss the characteristics of the various animals that inhabit the rain forest. Students can share group responses with the whole class after they have had time to meet in small groups.

How does the plight of the jaguar differ from that of the leopard?

What might happen if the harpy eagle, an integral part of the balance of nature in the tropical rain forest, became extinct?

If a sloth moves through the branches at one-half mile per hour, how long might it take for him to move to the next cecropia tree four miles away?

Discuss whether parrots can be bred humanely in captivity. Identify the advantages and disadvantages of buying a parrot that was bred this way.

Animal Information Cards

Chimpanzee

Scientists believe that of all wild animals, chimpanzees are our closest relative. Chimpanzees make their homes in the rain forests of Africa. They have been known to live in groups of up to 100 animals. The noisiest male is usually the group leader. Male chimpanzees often fight with one another. Female chimps are friendlier and get along well. Male chimps grow to be about five feet (1.52 m) tall and weigh about 110 pounds (50 kg). Female chimps are usually a little smaller. Chimps, like other apes, do not have tails.

Chimpanzees eat plants and meat. They are capable of killing pigs and antelope for food. Male chimps work in teams to trap monkeys in trees. When they are lucky enough to find a large amount of food, the males make drumming noises on the tree trunks to call other chimps to the feast.

Chimpanzees are very clever. They have learned how to use simple tools to get the food they want. They use sticks to crack nuts to get the juicy kernels inside and to catch tasty termites. Chimps have also been known to chew leaves, making them spongy, so they can use them to soak up water for drinking.

Quetzal

The quetzal of Southern Mexico and Central America is among the most beautiful birds in the world. The quetzal is also known as the royal bird of Costa Rica. Its body is green with highlights of gold and red. The black wings of the quetzal have splashes of white on them. The male quetzal is about 15 inches (38 cm) in length from head to tail. However, the long wisp of feathers beneath its tail add another 15 to 30 inches (38 to 76 cm) to the quetzal's length. The female quetzal is slightly less attractive. Her feathers are not as vibrant in color nor are they as long and graceful as her male counterpart's.

Quetzals are known to eat ants and wasps, but they mainly depend on the fruits of the wild avocado tree for nourishment. The quetzal is an endangered animal because excessive logging of the rain forest has resulted in the loss of many wild avocado trees.

The quetzal's great beauty has inspired people to incorporate it into their cultures in many ways. Often, rain forest native art and mythology have featured this royal bird. The ancient Mayans and Aztecs considered the quetzal to be a sacred creature. Today, the quetzal serves as the national symbol of Guatemala.

Animal Information Cards (cont.)

Macaw

Macaws are the world's largest parrots. There are several different kinds of spectacularly colored macaws, and they all live in South America. Macaws are seed predators rather than seed dispersers. They are able to eat the toughest fruits and seeds, even if they contain toxic chemicals.

Macaws have large, powerful bodies which protect them from being eaten by many bird predators. The macaw's hooked beak can open even the hardest nuts, like Brazil nuts, with ease. It uses the edge of the beak like a saw to cut partially through the shell, making it easy to complete the job. The top and bottom parts of the macaw's beak constantly rub against each other, keeping the edges sharp.

The macaw's beak is also useful as an extra foot when it is climbing through the trees. The macaw's foot has four toes. Two of these face forward, and two of them face backward. This enables the macaws to pick up objects and hold them tightly.

Parrots such as macaws make popular pets and are often taken into captivity. Although there are laws attempting to protect the parrots, poachers continue to illegally capture and sell these beautiful creatures.

Toucan

Some of the most distinctive birds that come from the tropical rain forests are toucans. Toucans have large, brightly colored beaks which are serrated and are displayed in courtship rituals. Toucan beaks are so large that they are sometimes longer than the toucan's body!

There are about 37 species of toucans, the largest of which is the Ramphastos. In general, the toucan's body is usually one to two feet (30 to 60 cm) in length. The plumage of these birds match their personalities; both are very loud. Sections of the vibrant colors such as red, yellow, and green contrast sharply with the mostly black or dark green feathers on the toucan's body. These colorful birds are supported by strong legs and feet which have two toes pointed forward and two toes pointed backward.

Toucans nest in the tree cavities of the Central and South American rain forests. In these nests, both toucan parents incubate and raise their offspring. Fruit makes up the bulk of the toucan diet.

Animal Information Cards *(cont.)*

Harpy Eagle

The tropical rain forest is the home to the world's largest and most ferocious eagle, the harpy eagle. This rare predator hunts high up in the jungle canopy. It sleeps at night and hunts by day. The harpy eagle is a very swift and agile flyer which enables it to chase monkeys through the jungle. Its gray feathers provide the eagle with a natural camouflage.

The harpy eagle makes its nest in the tallest emergent trees (most often the silk cotton trees). Usually, only one harpy eagle chick is successfully raised on the large platform of twigs used as a nest. It takes six months for the chick to reach adulthood.

The harpy eagle dines mainly on unsuspecting, sleeping sloths and chattering capuchin monkeys. Occasionally, their diet includes agouti, kinkajous, snakes, anteaters, large parrots, and small deer.

Caiman

Caimans are reptiles that are closely related to their Central and South American neighbors, the alligators. Adult caimans are usually four to six feet (1.2 m–1.8 m) in length. They have short legs and powerful tails which are used for both swimming and as weapons.

Caimans live along river banks where they patiently wait for thirsty animals to come for a drink—then, they attack their unsuspecting prey! They can float under the water with only their eyes, nostrils, and ears showing. A valve closes off the gullet of the windpipe so that the mouth can be opened under-water to eat its favorite food—fish. The caiman's greatest enemy is man.

Some caimans have been found to leave the river to lay their eggs next to termite nests. As the termites continue to build their nest, they surround the caiman's eggs. The nests keep half the eggs warm and half the eggs cool. The warm eggs develop into male caimans, and the cool eggs develop into females. When the baby caimans hatch, they head straight for the river where they spend their lives.

Animal Information Cards *(cont.)*

Gorilla

Because gorillas are the largest living primates, they are quite often misunderstood. They are usually represented as aggressive, violent, and short-tempered creatures, when in fact they are actually one of the most gentle primates in existence. These giants of the African rain forests can reach up to six feet (180 cm) in height and 400 pounds (180 kg) in weight. Despite their size, fighting among the gorillas is rare.

Contrary to popular belief, the gorillas are not carnivores (meat eaters), but rather they are herbivores (plant eaters). During the daytime they forage for food on the forest floor. Unlike other members of the ape family, most gorillas, due to their size, do not scour the tree tops in search of food or shelter.

Gorillas live and travel in family groupings. The family unit consists of one dominate silverback male (the term "silverback" comes from the gray fur on a mature male), one or two females, a few young males, and various juveniles. Gorillas are quadrupeds because they travel on all four limbs. They use the knuckles of their hands to help support their heavy upper bodies.

Tarsier

The tarsier lives in the rain forests of Indonesia, Malaysia, Brunei, and the Philippines. This Southeast Asian mammal is in danger of extinction because its forests are being destroyed. The tarsier is a rat-sized relative of the monkey.

This creature is one of the strangest looking primates, in large part because of its unique eyes, ears, and feet. Its body is only about six inches (15 cm) in length. The tarsier has long, powerful hind legs which allow it to leap up to 20 feet (6 meters). The pads on its toes and fingers help to hold on to branches. The tarsier's head can almost turn in a complete circle. This is a very important feature since the tarsier cannot move its eyes.

This animal spends most of its life living in the trees of the rain forest. It is, for the most part, nocturnal (active during the night and resting during the day), and it has large, sharp eyes that enable it to hunt all sorts of small animals at night. It leaps onto its prey (which is usually a lizard or an insect), catches the creature with its hands, and then kills it with its sharp teeth.

Animal Information Cards *(cont.)*

Fer-de-lance

The most feared poisonous snake found in Central and South America is called the fer-de-lance. This snake gets its name from the Creole-French language, and it means "head of a lance." A lance is a type of weapon that has a spearhead, which some people believe looks similar to the head of this snake. The fer-de-lance averages four to six feet (1.2 to 1.8 meters) in length but can grow up to seven feet (2.1 meters) long. Usually olive or dark brown in color, it has a pattern of dark-edged triangles on its skin.

Small depressions on its head mark a heat-sensing organ that helps the animal find its warm-blooded, mammalian prey by the heat the prey generates. The fer-de-lance protects itself by striking its enemy. Its venom quickly produces severe hemorrhaging and is lethal.

This snake lives in the understory or forest floor, hiding among the leaf litter, tree roots, and buttresses. It gives birth to live offspring and may produce as many as 70 young at one time.

Boa

Boas are nonpoisonous snakes. They kill their food by wrapping themselves around an animal and squeezing tightly until the animal dies from suffocation. Boas then stretch their jaws open extremely wide to swallow their prey whole. They are able to open their jaws so wide that they can actually swallow animals that are larger than their own heads.

There are about 70 species in the boa family which can be found worldwide. Unlike some other types of snakes who lay eggs, the boa gives birth to live offspring. Some kinds of boas never grow any longer than 24 inches (61 cm) while others, such as the boa constrictor, may grow as large as 14 feet (4 meters) in length.

One of the most beautiful snakes found in Central and South America is the emerald tree boa. Its green skin is striped with white or yellow, which camouflages it well in its home in the canopy layer. This protective coloration allows the snake to approach its prey without being seen and also helps it to avoid being eaten by its predators, one of which is the harpy eagle.

Animal Information Cards *(cont.)*

Lemur

Lemurs are distant cousins of monkeys. They are found only on the island of Madagascar. They have been able to survive there because of a lack of monkeys on the island that would be competing for the same food.

There are 15 different kinds of lemurs in Madagascar. Most of them are cat or squirrel-sized, but some, like the mouse lemur, are as small as five inches (12.7 cm) long and weigh only two ounces (56 g). The indri lemur is the biggest lemur, growing to over two feet (30 cm) long. It is able to make extraordinary leaps through the trees but, when on the ground, bounces on its big back legs.

Most lemurs roam the forest in small groups looking for food. They eat fruit, leaves, bark, and insects. Different types of lemurs are active during different times of the day. Some species are nocturnal (active at night), some are diurnal (active during the day), and some are active only at dusk.

The lemur population is dwindling. Some species of lemurs are in danger of extinction because the forests of Madagascar are rapidly being destroyed.

Aye-aye

The cat-sized aye-aye is an unusual and rare type of lemur. Its enormous eyes and rounded, hairless ears indicate that the aye-aye is nocturnal (it comes out at night). During the daytime it sleeps in hollow trees or among branches. The aye-aye is a very small animal, measuring only about 36 inches (91 cm) long; more than half of that length is due to its bushy tail.

The aye-aye is a loner. It hunts alone, using its long fingers to scoop out bamboo pith, sugar cane, beetles, and insect larvae. The curved, slender fingers are also used to comb its fur. Unfortunately for the aye-aye, the natives of Madagascar believe that these long fingers possess magical properties and bring good luck to the owners. Many aye-ayes have lost their lives because of this. Their fingers did not bring them good luck!

Aye-ayes can be found only on the island of Madagascar, and there are fewer than ten aye-ayes known to exist there. Aye-ayes are not found in any of the world's zoos; therefore, the only way we will probably ever view one is to look in a book.

Animal Information Cards *(cont.)*

Orangutan

Orangutans can be found only on the islands of Borneo and Sumatra in Southeast Asia. They were named "men of the woods" because their faces are so human-looking. Orangutans are wonderful climbers and spend most of their time in the treetops, swinging from branch to branch.

Like other apes, orangutans do not have tails. They have long red hair and strong arms. Their long toes help them grip the branches as they climb in the trees.

Orangutans have huge appetites. Their favorite food is fruit, but they will also eat leaves, shoots, tree bark and, occasionally, birds' eggs. Orangutans are very clever and have learned to follow fruit-eating birds to find their favorite food.

The orangutans have become very rare due to the loss of their habitat, the rain forest. Additionally, orangutans have been hunted, captured, and sold as pets. Special reserves have been set up to help the remaining orangutans survive.

Indian Elephant

Indian elephants are the largest animals in the rain forests of Asia, although their African cousins are larger. Elephants roam about in small herds. Their diet mainly consists of leaves which they pull from the trees and shove into their mouths, using their trunks.

The Indian elephant's two very large teeth are called tusks. These tusks consist of ivory. The females usually have smaller tusks than the males. Unlike the flat back of the African elephant, the Indian elephant has a strongly arched back. It has a domed forehead and a smooth trunk. It can weigh up to six tons (5.44 tonnes). The ears of the Indian elephant do not reach down as far as its mouth and are smaller than the ears of the African elephant.

Indian elephants have been trained as workers in the forests. They are better than machines when it comes to getting out big logs from between the trees. They can drag huge logs from the forest and pick them up with their trunks and tusks. The forests where they live are gradually being destroyed, and the irony of it is that the tamed, working elephants are helping to cause the damage.

Animal Information Cards *(cont.)*

Anteater

This tree-living, cat-sized anteater is also called a tamandua. It has short, coarse fur and a prehensile tail. South American tamanduas have honey-colored coats, while the Central American ones have bold, two-toned black and tan coats.

The tamandua has powerful claws that help it both in climbing and in getting food. It wraps its tail around tree limbs to hold on while it rips open ant and termite nests with its claws. It then catches the insects with its long sticky tongue, licking up thousands at one time. It will also eat other insects such as bees and beetles.

Contrary to common belief, the anteater does not eat all types of ants or termites! They avoid army ants because they are too aggressive and can sting. It also will not eat leaf cutter ants, as they are spiny and difficult to swallow in its long, toothless mouth. Azteca ants are a favorite of the tamandua, but the anteaters approach these nests very cautiously. After several minutes of eating these azteca ants, thousands more of them pour out from the nest, covering the tamandua and biting it with their tiny jaws, causing the tamandua to retreat.

Agouti

The agouti is a large, rabbit-sized rodent with a short tail and long legs. It is mainly active by day (diurnal), but is also active at dusk or at night (nocturnal). It lives on the forest floor and sleeps in burrows.

Agoutis have a very strange behavior called scatter-hoarding. Most rodents destroy all the seeds that they gather and eat; the agouti, however, carries seeds long distances and buries them whole.

There are some trees that produce seeds that are too heavy to be dispersed by bats or monkeys and have to rely on animals like agoutis for dispersal. Brazil nut fruits fall to the ground where their hard, woody shells are chiseled open by the agouti.

The agouti eats some of the seeds and scatter-hoard the rest. They do not usually find all the Brazil nut seeds that they bury; consequently, these seeds germinate and grow into new Brazil nut trees.

Animal Information Cards *(cont.)*

Sloth

The sloth does nearly everything upside down. Found in Central and South America, this slowest-of-all-mammals' top speed is one-half mile per hour. It lives its entire life in one cecropia tree, hanging by its huge hook-like claws. In addition to cecropia leaves, it eats flowers, fruit, and insects.

Its long, coarse, grayish-brown fur grows from its belly towards it back (the opposite of all other animals' fur), which enables the rain to run off easily, keeping the sloth dry in the wet rain forest. Nonetheless, its fur often appears a greenish color due to the algae that grow on it. In addition to the algae, the sloth's fur contains sloth moths, beetles, and mites. When the sloth descends to the forest floor, these insects utilize the sloth's dung to lay their eggs. Caterpillars also live on the sloth's fur and feed on the algae.

The sloth spends nearly its entire life among the trees' branches. It visits the forest floor about once every week or two to defecate, thereby fertilizing its own home. Once on the ground, the sloth cannot walk and must drag itself. However, during the rainy season, when the Amazon floods, sloths can swim from treetop to treetop.

Jaguar

The rarely seen jaguar is the largest predator of the dense forests of Central and South America. The jaguar is an excellent swimmer and climber and usually can be found close to water where it sleeps by day and hunts by night (a nocturnal animal). It prefers to eat large animals like wild pig or tapir, but, being an excellent hunter, its diet also includes sloths, snakes, mice, caimans, turtles, iguanas, and fish. The jaguar is the major predator of the lower levels of the rain forest.

The jaguar's coat is spotted like its cousin's, the leopard, but its rings are different. Nearly all of them have a spot in the middle. This camouflages the jaguar as he stalks through the jungle. Jaguars can weigh up to three hundred pounds (136 kg).

A number of disasters threaten these beautiful creatures. Jaguars have long been hunted for their luxurious fur. Although there are many laws protecting these creatures, illegal killing and smuggling of the jaguars' fur continues. As the population grows, rain forest land is being slashed and burned to clear land for ranching. This is causing a loss of habitat for many rain forest animals which the jaguar depends upon for food. Consequently, the jaguars have begun to feed on the ranchers' livestock. In turn, this has resulted in their being killed by the ranchers.

Content DR-TA (Directed Reading-Thinking Activity)

Read a children's book about the rain forest to your students and talk about the rain forest.

- Before reading, have students predict what the story will be about based on the title and the cover of the book and their background knowledge. Students can work with partners or in small groups to brainstorm ideas and list everything they know about the vegetation in their learning logs.

- The teacher announces a specific topic related to the book. Have students go back and check off the items on their lists that relate to this topic.

- Ask students to add to their lists new ideas that directly relate to the topic.

- After the teacher reads a few pages, students evaluate their predictions by circling the correct items they have on their lists. They can make new predictions before the teacher continues to read the next few pages.

- As a whole class, discuss predictions and outcomes and specific knowledge that was learned from the novel.

Becoming an Ethnobotanist

Name _____ Date_____

You are an ethnobotanist, a researcher who studies the native plants and their use by the local, indigenous peoples, specializing in the rain forests of the world. Your research project is to discover many different rare species of plants that live in the rain forests all over the world. In your research you want to compare the rain forests in South America and Central America and gather as much information as you can for an upcoming scientific conference in which you have been invited to be the guest speaker. You may gather scientific journal articles, photographs, or other artifacts throughout your research. You will take a two-week trip to visit the rain forests to collect authentic samples for further research. Keep a journal to record notes, comments, and questions that require further inquiry. Present your research findings to your class before you head off to your scientific research conference. Use the space below to write your beginning research ideas.

Phase One: The teacher reads a section of related text to the class, and you take notes and develop research ideas.

_____

_____

_____

_____

Phase Two: Make a list of appropriate sources (primary and secondary) you should read and then take notes. Write down questions that need further investigation.

_____

_____

_____

_____

Phase Three: Initiate and carry out research (for example, visit the library or appropriate Internet sites).

_____

_____

_____

_____

Weather and Temperature

Name _____ Date_____

On your trip to the rain forests to research the rare species of plants found in South American and Central American rain forests, chart the weather and temperature to determine why different plants grow in the different rain forests. Use this chart to draw conclusions and make predictions about the future of the plants and animals that live in the rain forest.

Location	Temperature	Weather	Predictions

Layers of the Rain Forest

Name _____ Date_____

The tropical rain forest is made up of a complex system of layers which includes trees, shrubs, vines, ferns, and many other rare species of plants. There are four layers of the rain forest: the *forest floor, understory, canopy*, and *emergent layer*. Since there is no distinct boundary between any of the four layers, as an ethnobotanist you must determine the boundaries which explain how the different species of plants are able to thrive in the varying conditions of each layer.

- Create a chart or a graph depicting your estimated measurements of each layer and an explanation of how the plants grow under specific conditions.

- Create a visual map of the layers of the rain forest.

- Create a semantic map explaining the relationships between the layers of the rain forest and the animals and plants that live within each layer. Use the space below for your semantic map.

Semantic Map

Analysis of Rain Forest Plants and Trees

Name _____ Date_____

In your ethnobotany research of the rare species of plants and trees that grow in the rain forests in South America and Central America, record the relationships among plants that live within the same layer. In the left column list all of the plants and trees that you have discovered in the South American rain forest and across the top identify environmental factors the plants or trees need in order to grow. Create another semantic feature analysis for the plants and trees that grow in the Central American rain forests. Then compare your results and explain the relationships between the environmental factors and plant growth in the rain forests in your research report.

Plants Found in South American Rain Forests

	Needs Sunlight	Needs Moisture	Produces Poison	Grows in the Shade
fern				
orchid				
kapok tree				

Plants Found in Central American Rain Forests

	Needs Sunlight	Needs Moisture	Produces Poison	Grows in the Shade
pineapple				
cepropia tree				
vines				

People of the Rain Forest

Name _____ Date_____

You will be reading a text selection about the people of the rain forest. As you read the passage, think about the following questions and develop thorough and complete answers. Record your answers in your learning logs.

- Create a semantic map to organize the information you already know and the new information you learn from reading the passage. Use the space below for your semantic map.

- Add new vocabulary words from the passage to your vocabulary log.

- Choose two or three words to nominate for the class vocabulary self-collection activity.

- How many different cultures of people live in the tropical rain forests?

- How do people learn to survive in the tropical rain forests?

- What can we learn from the people of the rain forest?

- Can we offer anything to these cultures?

Semantic Map

Rain Forest People

The tropical rain forest contains not only a multitude of animals and plants but people as well. Today, there are still hundreds of rain forest cultures that continue to live a lifestyle much like that of their ancestors.

These rain forest people live in harmony with their environment as the forest plays an integral part in their daily lives. The rain forest provides them with all of their necessities; in return, they honor and respect it as evidenced in their rituals.

While Western societies may look upon these rain forest cultures as primitive, in many ways they are far more knowledgeable and advanced than we are about the ability to function in their natural habitats. They know when certain fruits will ripen, when it is time for planting, and they work in harmony with the forest's natural cycles.

The indigenous people of the rain forest know more about the plants and animals of the rain forests than even the most educated scientists. In the Amazon Basin, for example, the indigenous people use over two thousand different plants as pharmaceuticals.

Modern ethnobotanists are furiously studying all they can about rain forest cultures and their use of the forest plants to treat their illnesses—before it is too late! Ethnobotany is the study of how indigenous people use local plants.

Rain forest cultures are quickly disappearing, and as they disappear, so does the opportunity for us to learn more about our world.

Many indigenous cultures have faced destruction through contact with the outside world. Rain forest people have not yet built up immunities to many diseases. Occupants of entire jungle villages have fallen ill and died from exposure to common diseases, some as ordinary as the flu.

Another threat to the lifestyle of the rain forest people is the pressure to assimilate into other cultures. Clothing, cooking pots, guns, and toys are being introduced as the modern world encroaches more and more on the rain forest world.

The new generation is less interested in the important lessons taught by their elders. Many are choosing to leave their cultures behind in their quest to join modern society.

Rain Forest People *(cont.)*

Pygmies of the Congo

Deep in the jungle of the Ituri Forest in the Congo live the Mbuti (mm-BOO-tee) Pygmies. These nomads, who hunt and gather their food to survive, live much as their ancestors did thousands of years ago. The Mbutis identify the rain forest as the provider of life and of all beneficial things, including food, shelter, and clothing. Additionally, they view the forest as their protector from non-forest people and all harmful things.

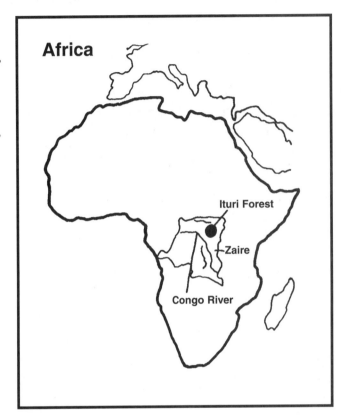

The Mbuti Pygmies take full advantage of whatever the forest has to offer. They sometimes hunt large game, such as elephants, okapis, and buffalo, but they mostly hunt smaller animals like monkeys and birds. The women provide most of the food the Pygmies eat, either by collecting it from the forest or working for it in the villages.

The Mbuti use bows and arrows or nets for hunting. In some Mbuti groups, hunting is a cooperative effort undertaken only by the men and boys. In other groups of Mbuti Pygmies, men, women, and children all participate.

Honey season is an integral part of Mbuti culture and one they look forward to each year. During the brief season, they consume an enormous amount of honey which accounts for much of their calorie intake during the year.

The Pygmies have two features that make them quite unique, their characteristic reddish-brown skin and their small stature. Pygmies grow to be only four to four and a half feet (1.2 to 1.4 m) tall.

The Pygmies live in groups comprised of several families. In general, it is the men who hunt and collect honey while the women fish, collect wood and water, gather berries, build huts, and prepare food. Pygmy women are also the primary caretakers of the children. The children develop adult survival skills through play. Boys begin to hunt with the male elders at about age nine. Girls are trained for their chores from age three.

The Mbuti Pygmies are beautiful in their simplicity. They are not burdened with too many possessions. The forest provides them with what they need to survive. They do not negatively impact the forest because they are few in number and do not stay in one place for long periods of time. This allows the forest to replenish itself.

Rain Forest People *(cont.)*
Wayana Indians

Living in scattered communities on the northern coast of South America are the Wayanas. This group of less than 1,000 Indians has survived for centuries in the remote rain forest of the Amazon region. Their settlements are so deep within the rain forest that they seldom see any sunlight. Canoes provide their only means of transportation along the Maroni and Itany Rivers.

The Wayanas once numbered over 3,000. It is believed they migrated to Guiana from northern Brazil. By 1950, due to exposure to measles and tuberculosis, there were fewer than 500 Wayanas left. Thanks to a medical program established by the French government in 1961, their numbers are increasing. Additionally, tourism was restricted in their area to reduce any future threat of epidemic diseases.

The Wayanas are a resourceful people who are expert in finding and collecting rain forest edibles. Iguana eggs are found by poking a stick into the river's sandy beaches. Smoked iguana meat produces a rich flavor to contrast with the sweet wild nuts and berries. Wild honey is gathered fresh from the comb, and crunchy, large ants are eaten alive. However, the Wayana's favorite treat is fat, juicy grubs!

Each family resides in its own home, which is raised high above the ground to protect it from rats and crawling insects. The furnishings are sparse and consist of hammocks made from webbed cotton. The hammocks are hung inside the houses at night and underneath, where it is shady, during the day.

Survival skills are taught to young children through play. Domestic chores are shared. Women traditionally prepare the manioc root to make food and drink. They also spin cotton which they weave into hammocks. The men usually construct the baskets and other straw goods. Authority and childcare are shared.

An interesting and unique Wayana custom is the "ant test" known as marake. Its purpose is to prepare young men and women for physical hardship. Marake begins with dancing, storytelling, and drinking kasili, a mild fermented brew made from manioc root. Then a wicker frame holding up to a hundred stinging ants is applied to all parts of the child's body. The child proves to be a true Wayana by remaining still and silent.

The simplicity of the Wayana way of life is being tested by the increasing pressures from the outside world. Alcoholism has become a serious family problem. How long the Wayana culture can withstand the infiltration of outside influences remains unknown. Suicide among teenagers, previously unknown to these people, is a sign of the changing times.

Rain Forest People *(cont.)*

The Penan of Borneo

Before deforestation, almost the entire island of Borneo in Southeast Asia was rain forest. In the northern part of the vast and lush Sarawak rain forest, a tribe called the Penan flourished for over 40,000 years.

The survival of the Penan depends upon hunting game and gathering fruits and nuts. Their entire diet is provided directly from nature. This has become increasingly more difficult due to the destruction of the rain forest. Food for the Penan is far more scarce than it once was.

To hunt, the Penans use blowpipes that stand taller than they do. They catch and eat wild boar (their staple meat), monkeys, deer, and hornbills. The blowpipe is loaded with a dart dipped in poison that is derived from tree sap. The poison is forcefully blown through the pipe towards the unsuspecting prey. When used for fishing, the end of the blowpipe is fitted with a spear.

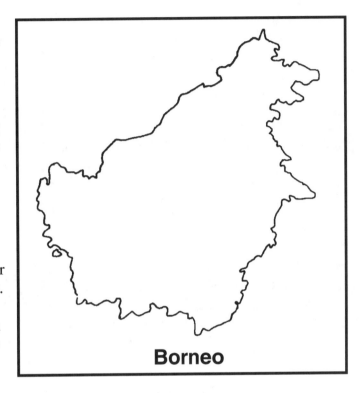

Borneo

Being nomadic people, the concept of land ownership is totally foreign to them. Like so many other rain forest people, they move freely around the rain forest as they hunt game and gather foods and natural medicines. That is, they did until the logging companies arrived!

Malaysian and foreign lumber companies, with government approval, have cut down trees in the forest. The Penan were forced to live in villages of 800 people or more. This was a major adjustment for people used to living in smaller family groups of only 20 to 30. No longer can they freely wander through the beautiful forest. Instead, in these new villages, they suffer from malnutrition and diseases they never before faced.

Logging has driven away the animals and, consequently, disrupted the hunting and fishing of the Penan. Furthermore, without trees, there is nothing to prevent the soil from flowing into the rivers during heavy rains. The rivers, therefore, have become saturated with silt, making fishing difficult.

The Penan, being a peaceful tribe, attempted to protect their way of life by erecting a blockade across the logging road at Long Ajeng. After nine months of resistance, the Malaysian government's response was to send in 1,000 riot police to force the Penan to remove the blockade. Many Penan were arrested. The logging companies were given free rein to reenter the land of the Penan without regard for the survival of the people.

Once 10,000 strong, the Penan, now only a few thousand, face an uncertain future.

Rain Forest People (cont.)

The People of the Amazon

More rain forest land is destroyed in Brazil than in any other country of the world. Since Brazil's rain forests were so huge, it still has more rain forest land remaining than any other country. About one-third of the world's rain forest acreage is in Brazil.

Sadly, about two percent of Brazil's remaining rain forests are cut or burned each year. If this present rate of destruction continues, in 50 years all of Brazil's rain forests will be gone.

In 1975, the Brazilian government opened an unpaved two-lane road through their rain forests. It was hoped that this Transamazon Highway would give millions of poor people in Brazil a place to live and allow companies to take advantage of the natural resources of the Amazon basin.

The road has helped the Brazilian economy but has been disastrous for the rain forest.

Brazil

The road allowed farmers and ranchers to remove trees to create fields and pastures. Miners looking for gold have also arrived. The gold mining activities pollute the many rivers of the Amazon region with highly toxic metals. Gold mining depletes the rain forest and pollutes the air because it entails burning enormous amounts of wood.

In 1987, gold miners brought disease to the Yanomani natives. Within three years, 15% of the population had died of tuberculosis, malaria, mumps, flu, or the common cold. Fishing in the Yanomani's rivers has been ruined by the mercury used to extract gold. The mercury now contaminates their waters, their lands, and even the people themselves.

Of the sixteen million people living in the Brazilian Amazon, only 200,000 are indigenous. Mining roads, logging, and ranching are eroding the rain forest people's very existence. The Urueu-Wau-Wau of Rondonia and the Waimiri-Atroari of the central Brazilian Amazon number only a few hundred people today compared with thousands in the 1970s. A project called Calha Norte, designed to bring more development into the remote jungle, is largely responsible.

Similar catastrophes for indigenous tribes are occurring in rain forests everywhere. In Chile, the Mapuche Indians face economic, health, and human rights problems. In Panama, the Guaymis suffer from land takeovers by Panamanian cattle ranchers. In Ecuador, road and oil pipeline construction threaten the peaceful way of life for the Waorani. This same sad story is being retold again and again in the tropical rain forests around the world.

Rain Forest Vocabulary Log

Name _____ Date_____

Here is a start for your rain forest vocabulary log. Make sure you write the definition for each word and use it in a sentence or draw illustrations so you will not forget it! Continue to add words as you learn more about the rain forest.

algae	bromeliad	canopy
ecology	endangered species	food chain
greenhouse effect	reforestation	understory

Rain Forest Double-Entry Journal

Name _____ Date_____

Why should we save the rain forests?

_____

_____

_____

_____

_____

_____

_____

List reasons why we should continue our efforts to save the tropical rain forests around the world.

_____

_____

_____

_____

_____

_____

_____

Write your own ideas, comments, questions, and pictures that help you to understand more about the tropical rain forest and why we should save it.

_____

_____

_____

_____

_____

_____

_____

_____

_____

_____

_____

_____

_____

_____

_____

_____

_____

_____

Guided Writing Prompts

Directions: Use the following writing prompts to express your ideas relating to the tropical rain forest.

On your journey to the tropical rain forests in South America and Central America you discover a new species of plants that is destroying the rain forest. What do you do?

Imagine that a jaguar attacks you and your research assistant is trying to get you help. What will you both do?

The Wayana Indians capture you and your research assistant. What happens to you during your captivity, and how do you escape?

If you were allowed to bring back only one artifact from your research trip, what would it be and why?

Section III
Generic Forms and
Bibliography

Concept Web

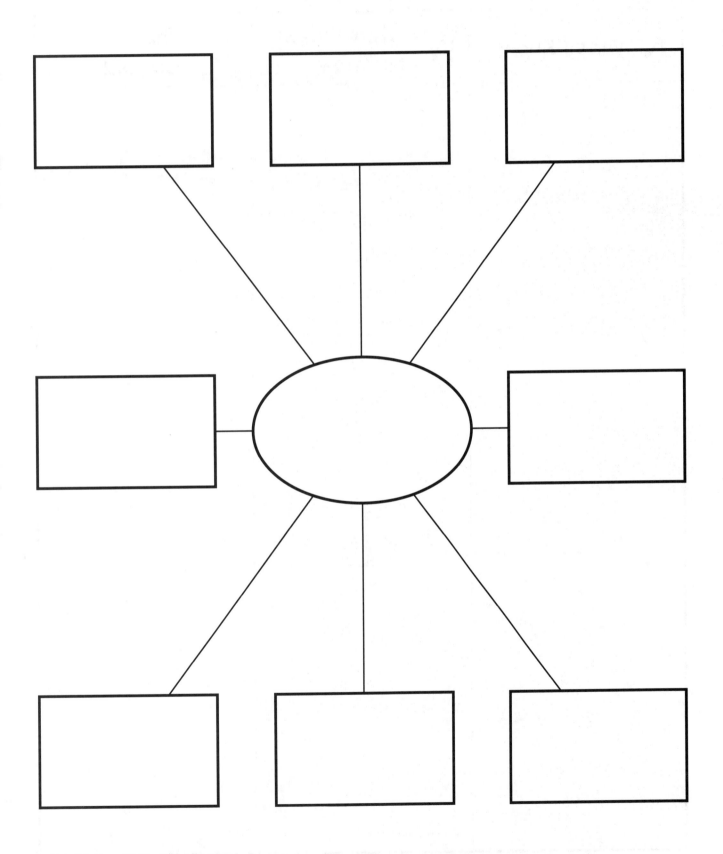

K-W-L Chart

K What I Know	W What I Want to Know	L What I Learned

Vocabulary Log

Name _____ Date_____

Here is a start for your vocabulary log. Make sure you write the definition for each word and use it in a sentence or draw illustrations so you will not forget the word. Use more copies of this page as you add words you have learned in this unit.

word	definition	illustration
	_____	
_____	_____	
word	_____	
	_____	
	_____	

word	definition	illustration
	_____	
_____	_____	
word	_____	
	_____	
	_____	

word	definition	illustration
	_____	
_____	_____	
word	_____	
	_____	
	_____	

Word Sleuth

Name _____ Date_____

Topic/Situation:

As a word sleuth, your job is to collect and investigate the origins and meanings of the following words, terms, phrases, etc. Use the chart below to collect your information.

Word	Origin	Meaning

Double-Entry Journal

Name _____ Date_____

Topic: _____

Initial Prompts	**Revised Ideas/New Insights**

Conceptual Relationships

Name _____ Date_____

Main Concept

Use this page to explain the relationships among the main concept and the other ideas, people, places and events you have added to your concept web. Be sure to make the connection and the integration clear so as you add more information you do not become confused.

My ideas are connected to the main concept in the following ways:

_____

_____

_____

_____

_____

_____

_____

_____

_____

_____

_____

_____

_____

_____

_____

_____

Bibliography

Atwell, N. (Ed.) (1990). *Coming to know: Writing to learn in the intermediate grades.* Portsmouth, NH: Heinemann.

Blake, M. (1990). *Learning logs in the upper elementary grades.* In N. Atwell (Ed.), Coming to know: Writing to learn in the intermediate grades (pp. 53–60). Portsmouth, NH: Heinemann.

Calkins, L. M. (1994). *The art of teaching writing.* (2nd ed.) Portsmouth, NH: Heinemann.

Carr, El, & Ogle, D. (1987). *K-W-L Plus: A strategy for comprehension and summarization.* Journal of Reading (pp. 30, 626–631).

Chard, N. (1990). *How learning logs change teaching.* In N. Atwell (Ed.) Coming to know : Writing to learn in the intermediate grades (pp. 61–68). Portsmouth, NH: Heinemann.

Davidson, J.L. (1982). *The group mapping activity for instruction in reading and thinking.* Journal of Reading (pp. 26, 52–56).

Farnan, N. (1992). *Promoting connections between reader and text: A reader response approach.* The California Reader (pp. 25,6–8).

Graves, D. H. (1983). *Writing: Teachers and children at work.* Portsmouth, NH: Heinemann.

Haggard, M.R. (1985). *An interactive strategies approach to content reading.* Journal of Reading (pp. 29, 204–210).

Haggard, M.R. (1989). *Instructional strategies for developing student interest in content area subjects.* In D. Lapp, J. Flood, & N. Farnan (Eds.), Content area reading/learning: Instructional strategies (pp. 70–80), Englwood Cliffs, NJ: Prentice-Hall.

Maxim, D. (1990). *Beginning researchers.* In N. Atwell (Ed.) Coming to know: Writing to learn in the intermediate grades (pp. 3-16). Portsmouth, NH: Heinemann.

O'Flahavan, J. (1989). *An exploration of the effects of participant structure upon literacy development in reading group discussion* (Doctoral dissertation, University of Illinios at Urbana-Champaign.

Prenn, M. C. , & Honeychurch, J.C. (1990). *Enhancing content area learning through expressive writing.* In N.L. Cecil (Ed.) Literacy in the 90's (pp. 114–121). Dubuque, IA: Kendall/Hunt.

Raphael, T. E. (1982). *Question-answering strategies for children.* The Reading Teacher, (pp. 36, 186–190).

Raphael, T.E. (1986). *Teaching question-answer relationships, revisited.* The Reading Teacher, (pp. 39, 516–523).

Rosenblatt, L.M. (1978). *The reader, the text, the poem: The transactional theory of the literary work.* Carbondale, IL: Southern Illinois Press.

Bibliography (cont.)

Ruddell, M.R. (1993). *Teaching content area reading and writing.* Boston: Allyn & Bacon.

Ruddell, R.B., and Ruddell, M.R. (1995). *Teaching children to read and write: Becoming an influential teacher.*

Stauffer, R.G. (1976). *Teaching reading as a thinking process.* New York: Harper & Row.

Thomas, K.J. (1986). *The Directed Inquiry Activity: An instructional procedure for content reading.* In E. K. Dishner, T. W. Bean, J.E. Readence, & D.W. Moore (Eds.) Reading in the content areas (2nd ed.) (pp. 278–281). Dubuque, IA: Kendall/Hunt.

Vaughn, C.L. (1990). *Knitting writing: The Double-Entry Journal.* In N. Atwell (Ed.) Coming to know: Writing to learn in the intermediate grades. Portsmouth, NH: Heinemann.

Children's Literature

Filipovic, Z. (1994). *Zlata's diary: A child's life in Sarajevo.* Viking Penguin.

Frank, A. (1967). *Anne Frank: The Diary of a Young Girl.* New York: Doubleday.

Houston, J.W. & Houston, J.D. (1974). *Farewell to Manzanar.* New York: Bantam Book.

Martin, B. & Archambault, J. (1987). *Knots on a Counting Rope.* New York: Henry Holt.

TCM Resources for Content Area Units

064 *Share the Olympic Dream* by Aileen Cantwell and Mike Shepard (pages 12, 13, 15, 16, 21, 22, 24, 26, 27, 72, 73, 79-84, 128–134) Published by Teacher Created Materials, Inc. and Griffin Publishing

559 *A Guide for Using Anne Frank: The Diary of a Young Girl in the Classroom*—Guide written by Mari Lu Robbins (pages 20, 21, 26, 27)

574 *Ancient Egypt* by Michelle Breyer (pages 10–15, 17, 19, 37, 38, 43-49, 118–120, 126–131)

581 *World War II* by Julie Strathman (pages 30, 57-60, 66)

605 *Heroes* by Betty Burke and Janet Cain (pages 30, 57–60, 66)

674 *Rain Fores*t by Illene Miller and Laurie Agopian (pages 7–9, 18, 30–39, 84–88)

934 *Integrating Technology into the Curriculum* by Mary Hellen Bryant (pages 105–109)